DATE DUE

SEP 06 2012	shing
OCT 1 3 2016	
JAN 1 0 2018	

Better Bass Fishing

Secrets from the Headwaters
by a *Bassmaster* Senior Writer

Robert U. Montgomery

The Countryman Press
Woodstock, Vermont

ISBN: 978-0-88150-849-9

Cover Design by Rob Johnson, Johnson Design
Cover photo by Robert U. Montgomery
Interior photographs by the author unless otherwise specified
Composition by Faith Hague Book Design

Published by The Countryman Press, P.O. Box 748, Woodstock, VT 05091

Distributed by W. W. Norton & Company, Inc., 500 Fifth Avenue, New York, NY 10110
Printed in the United States of America

10 9 8 7 6 5 4 3 2 1

*To Joe, Merv, and Jim, adults who took me fishing when
I was young. To Ray Scott, who started it all, and to Dave Precht,
who gave me a chance and showed me the way.*

Contents

1

The Source

*L*ake Seminole, a prolific bass fishery of 37,500 acres, sprawls along the Florida-Georgia border. Its origin, however, lies hundreds of miles to the north, as a tiny trickle in the mountains of north Georgia.

Along its way, the tiny spring acquires tributaries and runoff, growing into the mighty Chattahoochee River. Before it reaches Seminole, it also is harnessed to form lakes Lanier, West Point, and Eufaula.

The Colorado, the Columbia, the Mississippi, the Missouri, the Ohio, and all their riverine impoundments have similar origins. So, too, do the rest of our rivers, lakes, and reservoirs. It is the way of bass fishing. We owe our sport to the source, to the headwaters where it all begins.

The mighty Chattahoochee River begins as a trickle in the mountains of Georgia.

This book sprang from headwaters as well. It took life at a farm pond, on a Cub Scouts outing 50 years ago. I didn't catch a fish on that first trip, but seeing others do it was enough to hook me for life.

The passion picked up speed from there, fed by fishing trips, fishing magazines, and a career with BASS that has been blessed by opportunities to explore the world's best waters with the world's best anglers.

The constant flow has brought me to this place in my life and to this book. Only instead of being filled with bass as a river or lake would be, the book contains secrets of how to catch them and how to make bass fishing a richer experience for you individually and for all of us collectively.

Want to know why the pros catch more bass than you? I will tell you that and help you improve.

Want to know how to catch not only more bass but bigger bass? I will tell you that, too.

And, just as important, I'll provide you with plenty of reasons to enjoy each and every day on the water, no matter what the fish are doing. For me, that's what "better bass fishing" truly is all about.

I've learned from the best during my 22 years as a senior writer for ESPN's *Bassmaster* magazine, the world's largest-circulation fishing magazine and the world's foremost authority on bass fishing. I've fished with the pros, talked with the pros, and struck out with the pros. I've picked their brains and watched them in action.

In addition, I've fished with and interviewed some of the best guides and recreational anglers around, from the Columbia River in the West to the Potomac in the East, from the backcountry lakes of Canada in the North to the big-bass fisheries in Mexico.

I've fished with and interviewed lure designers, too, learning why some baits work better than others and how some are designed more to catch anglers than fish.

I've interviewed fisheries biologists and researchers about bass intelligence and behavior.

In short, I know bass and bass fishing, and not just such technical stuff as what kind of rod to pair with your reel when fishing suspended jerkbaits. I know bass biology. I know strategies to improve your catch rate. I know how the weather affects fishing and why. I know what the pros know—and more.

I've been a good student over the years. That's confirmed by the fact that I've caught 10 bass that weighed more than 10 pounds each, including two that weighed 12. I've caught dozens of 8- and 9-pounders. When press anglers still competed during practice days at the Bassmaster Classic, I twice caught the biggest fish in the media division. A few fishing partners have accused me of being one of the "luckiest" anglers they've ever met.

And maybe I am—lucky to have fished with and learned from the best and then applied that knowledge for my own success.

This book will help you be lucky, too. You'll find out not only what I've learned from the pros, the guides, the lure designers, and the fisheries biologists, but also what I've discovered as I applied, and sometimes altered, that information for my own success. You then can do the same as you become a better bass angler.

"Anybody can improve," says Ray Scott, founder of BASS and my friend for more than 20 years. "Not everyone can be as talented as Kevin VanDam, but everyone can get better."

Here is one of my best secrets, one that's sure to help you be a better bass angler:

"Confidence" baits sometimes are more an accident of timing than they are truly superior lures.

Every bass angler has a confidence bait, or sometimes two or three. It is the "go-to" bait when the bass won't seem to bite anything else. It

BASS founder Ray Scott (cowboy hat) believes that every angler can improve. He is on the weigh-in stand at the Bassmaster Classic with former tournament director Dewey Kendrick (left) and pro angler Bernie Schultz.

has become the favorite because the anglers grew up throwing it, or first tried it on a day when the fishing was tough and it produced.

Using a confidence bait gives you a psychological boost, and that's important when the bite is slow—maybe more important than the bait itself. It heightens your concentration and makes you more eager to fish. It makes you more attentive to where you are casting and to detecting subtle bites. In short, throwing a confidence bait makes you a better angler.

SECRET If you don't have a confidence bait, work on developing a couple. You'll be a better bass angler for it.

But also don't forget that many, many variables play into whether a bass is going to bite your bait. Some we understand. Some we think that we understand. And some we don't even know about. That watery world below the surface is so different from ours that we simply cannot know it in the same way that we know our air environment.

Once in awhile, we really do catch bass because we have chosen the "right" bait. Other times, they hit because they are in an aggressive, feeding mode, or because we have found a concentration of fish that stirs itself into a competitive frenzy when a lure passes through. At such times, just about anything in your tackle box might work.

SECRET So, when you are catching bass on a confidence bait (or a new lure that you just bought at the store), pay attention to more than just what is tied on the end of your line, its color, and the way it moves in the water. Look at water depth and clarity. Determine where the bites occur in relation to cover, structure, and current. Note the weather conditions and wind direction.

In other words, benefit from the confidence that throwing a favorite bait gives you, but also be smart enough to realize that bass probably aren't biting it because it's your favorite or because it is vastly superior to others. Likely, they are biting because of a complex combination of favorable variables, of which the lure is just one.

I've shared these secrets with you in the beginning because they are some of the most important. Now you, like the pros, know that catching bass rarely is just about using the right bait.

Additional secrets will explain more about what the pros and nation's best guides have learned about the water, the weather, and the many other factors that influence bass behavior, and how they use that knowledge to catch more bass.

Others will help you find bass, a prerequisite if you are going to catch them.

Some will deal with specifics about rods, reels, line, baits, and casting and retrieval techniques. Many are short and to the point:

SECRET Round-edge baits and baits without legs and tails are much easier to skip under docks. Those with sharp edges and/or appendages dig into or stick onto the surface of the water, slowing them down and limiting their effectiveness.

Or here's one that the pros follow religiously, but others often neglect:

SECRET Always keep your rod in position for a hookset.

Many anglers absentmindedly shift their rod tips higher and higher as they fish, especially with soft plastics and topwaters. Then, when a bass bites, they can't generate enough power to drive home the hook.

Still other secrets will help you better care for yourself on and off the water, since a healthy and energetic angler will catch more bass than one who is not. And, finally, some will reveal how and where to catch the trophy bass of a lifetime.

You won't find this unique combination of bass fishing secrets anywhere else. After you've read and applied the contents of this book, I promise that you will be a better bass angler, and I hope that you also will join me in recognizing that every day on the water is among life's greatest riches.

Author's note: Pros, guides, and others provided secrets to me with the understanding that I would acknowledge their generous contributions. Therefore, I am including their names following the secrets that they shared with me—and you. Others originated with research for articles published in *Bassmaster* magazine and *BASS Times*. The remainder evolved directly from my own experiences and observations while on the water.

2

Biology and Behavior

During a day on the water together, Rick Clunn explained a philosophy to me that has made him one of the most successful bass tournament anglers of all time.

Among some tribes of Native Americans, he said, a boy first had to hunt and kill an animal with his hands before he was allowed to use weapons. To do that meant that he had to quietly stalk the animal so that he could observe its behavior. As he studied it, he noted it strengths and its weaknesses, and, with the latter, he developed a strategy for the kill. Also, in learning about his quarry, he developed a respect for it as another living being.

Of course, catching a fish without a rod and reel is a skill best left to bears. But the idea that you will be a better angler if you know about bass behavior is directly related to the Native American approach, and it is a strategy that has worked well for Clunn, as evidenced by his enduring success on the tournament trail.

SECRET You're just outsmarting yourself if you try to "outthink" bass. Yes, bass are capable of learned behavior. But they definitely aren't the Einsteins of the fish world. Carp and bluegill rank higher in laboratory tests. Most important, though, bass (and other fish species) don't "think," and they aren't "smart."

Rather, bass are selective as to food, cover, and water, and each spring they are driven by the biological imperative to spawn. Those anglers who are smart enough to recognize those needs and respond accordingly are the ones who catch the most and largest bass. They look for water and cover that they have learned is attractive to bass during each season of the year. They learn the migration routes that fish take to those locations. They observe what bass are feeding on and try to offer baits that are similar in appearance.

SECRET Although bass are not smart, they do seem to learn to avoid some baits. That's why new baits—and new colors, to a lesser degree—seem to produce better than older styles. For awhile. We saw it happen with buzzbaits in the 1980s and soft jerkbaits in the 1990s. Then came Senkos, swimbaits, and, more recently, chatterbaits and frogs.

SECRET The plastic worm (and possibly its many cousins in assorted shapes and sizes) seems to be the only bait that bass do not learn to avoid. Probably that is why it remains the most used artificial bait by anglers of all abilities.

Most of today's professionals, though, prefer faster-moving baits so that they can cover more water. They switch to soft plastics if the bass aren't actively feeding, or if they seem to want a subtler, slow-moving bait. They also keep soft plastics rigged and ready to use as "follow-up" baits when bass charge, but won't hit, spinnerbaits, crankbaits, or topwaters.

SECRET No matter how fast the gear ratio of your reel and how fast your retrieve, you can't get a bait away from a bass if it wants it. At best, you are reeling at 2 to 3 miles an hour, while a bass can swim at bursts of 12 to 18 miles an hour. So even if you are "burning" a bait, catching it requires just a jog for a bass.

The Bite

Anglers never should overlook the power of provocation, according to Ray Scott, founder of BASS and father of competitive bass fishing. That lesson was emphatically driven home to him while on Alabama's Lake Eufaula with Harold Sharp, his longtime tournament director.

"I was fishing the front and running the trolling motor," Ray remembers. "Harold was in the back and yet somehow he was catching twice as many bass as I was. Finally, I asked him what his secret was.

"He said, 'You're making them mad and then I'm catching them.'

"There's no other fish in the world like a bass," Ray continues, "and many times provocation is more important than 'Let's have lunch.' Yes, bass eat when they're hungry, but they also strike to protect their territory. I've seen a bass hit a bait, then swim a little ways and spit it out. It's a primary instinct.

"But you have to remember that what provokes that bass won't stay the same. It could change in 2 minutes or 10 days. And it's not because they think that we're trying to catch them. They're just doing what bass do.

"The guy who slows down and studies the fish, who can put the numbers together to figure them out, will do better than the others."

SECRET Fisheries scientists estimate that only 5 percent of fish in any given bass population are actively feeding at one time. Thirty percent are inactive, and 65 percent are neutral. That's why accurate casts, subtle presentations, and enticing retrieves are so important.

SECRET But even if a bass isn't "actively" feeding, it still often will grab at an easy meal if it comes within reach. Most of the time, fish and other wild animals simply do not pass up available food. Survival instinct dictates that they take advantage of every opportunity.

SECRET On average, once a largemouth bass reaches 11 inches in length, more than 75 percent of its diet consists of baitfish, with the remainder consisting of crayfish and insects. That will vary, of course, depending on the forage base of each specific fishery.

SECRET Bass bite for other reasons too, among them reflex, curiosity, competition, and protective instinct for their spawning beds and/or territory.

Longtime pro Roland Martin believes that they also bite out of ignorance: "It's getting increasingly harder to find bass these days that have never seen an artificial lure," he says. "But there are still a lot of lakes in Mexico and Canada where these 'ignorant' bass exist. And I've been able to find a few small farm ponds that were underfished and contained the same eager, stupid bass."

SECRET Bass, like all other predators, will feed on the largest available prey that requires the least amount of energy to catch and subdue.

Bass often will feed on the largest prey available. Sometimes, though, they try to swallow too much. This bass died trying to eat a tilapia that was too big.

At least that's what many resource managers believe, and they call this idea the "optimum foraging theory."

But don't be misled and believe that this means you always should throw big baits and retrieve them as slowly as possible if you want to catch large bass. You might see your magnum crankbait or 1-ounce spinnerbait as just what the big fish should want. But what you should be paying attention to is what the bass actually are feeding on. That's what they see as the best bang for their buck in terms of least amount of work for the best meal.

Slowing down your retrieve, however, almost always is a good idea if the bite is slow, especially if you're throwing a topwater or spinnerbait.

SECRET One of the most important discoveries that we've made from bass tournaments is that fish always can be caught somewhere, some way in a lake or river, even under the worst of conditions. In other words, the fact that you aren't catching them doesn't mean that no one else is either. Don't stick with a pattern or place too long if you aren't getting bites, especially if you are fishing a tournament and are limited by time.

SECRET While you can catch bass year-round, you will not, on average, boat as many bass in cold water as you do in warm. That's because bass are cold-blooded. At 39 degrees Fahrenheit, a bass's metabolism and digestion fall to only 20 percent and 10 percent, respectively, of what they were at 64 degrees.

SECRET Some bass *are* more difficult to catch than others. Researchers have proven this in their quest to develop strains of bass that are easier to catch for stocking in urban fisheries. In small ponds, they kept track of how many times each bass was caught and then bred together those most easily fooled. Offspring of those fish also proved easy to catch, suggesting that genetics play a role in whether a bass falls for an artificial.

SECRET Many anglers believe that Florida strain largemouth bass are more difficult to catch than northern strains. If that's true, it's probably because most of the waters in the Florida strain's natural range are shallow. That can make for some awesome fishing when conditions are right.

But it also means you'll get the cold shoulder when trying to catch them during or just after a cold front. Without deepwater refuges where they might be more inclined to bite, Florida bass often move in tight to protective shallow cover during cold weather and become very lethargic. Just about the only way to provoke a bite during such times is to drop a jig or soft plastic bait on the fish's nose.

Even in the deeper waters of Texas, Louisiana, California, and other places where they have been introduced, Florida strain largemouths still tend to "shut off" more completely during cold weather than do their northern counterparts.

SECRET Sight is the most important sense for a bass in finding food. That's why, when given a choice, it will move to clearer water to feed. And that's why you should seek out clear water too, especially in fisheries where most of the water is stained or muddy.

Bass feed year-round, but they are cold-blooded. That means their metabolism slows down as the weather and water cool.

Bass pro Ken Cook, a former fisheries biologist, has this to say about how bass see: "Underwater, a bass's eye is far superior to the human eye, probably so much better that we can only imagine what its capabilities are. Some studies have indicated that bass can see up to 12 times as well in muddy water as the human eye can in the same conditions."

SECRET But also check out muddy or stained water pouring into a lake, especially if it is warmer than the main body of water. The runoff contains insects, which attract forage fish, and they, in turn, attract bass.

SECRET Bass often will follow this discharge of warmer, stained water out into the lake, and you should, too.

SECRET Sometimes, muddy water is just on the surface, with clear water below. For instance, that can happen when a smaller, rain-filled tributary empties into a larger stream. Sometimes you can catch bass that are using the surface mud as ambush cover.

SECRET Bass don't see artificial baits the same way that we do. That new shad-shaped crankbait that you bought might look so lifelike that you expect it to flop off the table. But what makes it lifelike—and attractive—to bass is how it moves through the water. Yes, a realistic appearance helps, but good action that imitates an injured or fleeing baitfish probably is more important. That's why spinnerbaits, which don't resemble any kind of living creature when motionless, are such effective bass catchers.

SECRET With soft plastics, however, sometimes action isn't important at all. Rather, the fish need time to approach and examine. On several occasions, I've spent a minute or two picking out a backlash and then found a bass on the end of my line. Others have told me of similar experiences. This tells me that, too often, we fish soft plastics too quickly.

SECRET In fact, lure designer and tournament angler Troy Gibson recommends letting a soft plastic sit for 120 seconds after you cast it.

"I will find the fish by power fishing with spinnerbaits and crankbaits," he says. "And sometimes this is all I need to fill the livewell.

"But when I come across an area that looks as if it will produce 3- to 5-pound fish, then I will slow down with a fluke or worm and be very patient. I will present my lure to a tree, bush, or creek channel and let the bait sit still for at least 120 seconds.

"The bass is just like an old cat that cannot leave well enough alone and will pick up, move, eat, or play with the fluke or sinking worm. It can't help itself, for that is its nature. Understanding that, along with patience, will make you a much better fisherman.

Bass don't see artificial baits the same way we do. Action is what makes lures lifelike for them. This is why spinnerbaits are so effective.

"By doing this, I am more likely to cull the first five fish with larger fish. To me, the smaller fish that I caught by power fishing are the locator fish for areas that are holding the larger fish."

SECRET To obtain the most up-to-date information on bass biology and behavior, as well as new strategies for catching them, read *Bassmaster* magazine and *BASS Times*, both publications of ESPN/BASS. These are the most authoritative sources on bass fishing in the world. Many of today's young pros say that they grew up reading *Bassmaster*, and the knowledge they gained from the magazine was critical to their success.

Hot Spots

SECRET Most hot spots aren't static. That's because fish shift their positions as current, winds, and other variables change. For example, you might catch fish on the backside of a stump row, but later come back to find empty water. Possibly those bass have moved a few feet to a nearby breakline. Don't fall into the rut of casting to the same spots in the same way every time and then moving on if you don't get bites right away. Those fish might be feeding in deeper—or shallower—water just a cast away.

SECRET In general, finding the right locations is more important during summer and winter. That's because bass tend to school and stay in the same places for days or even weeks during these seasons. By contrast, lure selection can be more important during spring and fall. Fish roam more then, looking for places to spawn and chasing bait in the shallows.

SECRET With a full moon and water temperatures in the mid-60s, bass will be spawning in those shallows. But don't forget that not all bass will be in there at the same time. Some will be in deeper water, waiting their turns. Others won't spawn at all.

SECRET Ninety percent of bass anglers fish within 30 feet of shore and no deeper than 10 feet. But the pros know that finding concentrations of fish is a key to winning tournaments, and those concentrations more often are found in deeper water around structure and cover.

SECRET Understanding the terminology will make you a wiser and more successful angler. "Structure" is part of the topography of a lake, reservoir, or river, and includes drop-offs, ledges, and humps. "Cover" refers to aquatic vegetation, timber, brushpiles, rocks, and manmade fish attractors. Bass typically relate more to deep-water structure during winter and summer and more to shallow-water cover during spring and fall.

Brushpiles and timber provide some of the best bass-holding cover.

SECRET No matter what kind of cover or structure you are fishing, think "edges." As ambush predators, bass want a place that they can hide in, but can get into and out of quickly.

SECRET Edges aren't always on the outside. In a grass bed, for example, small open areas on the inside can be good places to catch bass.

SECRET If every place you look you see promising cover for bass,

Grass is almost always a good place to look for bass.

pick out the irregularities, and focus on them first. Look for places where different kinds of vegetation meet, or where rocks turn into pebbles. Look for the cover that has the deepest water nearby.

SECRET In fact, one of the best places to find a big bass is cover with quick and easy access to deep water.

SECRET Bass often will stack up in the backs of coves, when runoff from spring rains is pouring in. That's because it warms the water, washes in insects, and stirs up microorganisms for shad and other forage species to eat. The baitfish, of course, attract bass and other predators.

SECRET When exploring new waters for spotted bass, check out the bridges. They afford great cover at a variety of depths.

SECRET Submerged roadbeds are some of the finest fish-holding structures known to bass anglers. But not all roadbeds will be productive. The key is concentrating on the old roads that are different and have some type of irregularity. A super spot can be a roadbed that has good definition with adjacent ditches and culverts.

"Once I locate a roadbed, I spend several minutes closely examining it with my Pinpoint depth finder, looking for an irregular feature on it. If it is at the right depth, the best place on it is usually where it crosses a creek, drain, or small river channel," says pro angler Walt Reynolds. "On an improved road, you will usually find at least a culvert or two and possibly a bridge. Most culverts and bridges are reinforced with concrete or steel, so when you pass over them you will see a very definite echo on your depth finder. Be sure you mark the sweet spot with your GPS for easier finding later."

SECRET "When surrounded by cover, look for horizontal features." —Rick Lillegard, pro angler

Those features include fallen logs and submerged grass beds, as opposed to standing timber and bulrushes or cattails. All can be good, but horizontal cover likely will be more productive.

SECRET "If a lake has grass, key on it first, regardless of the time of year." —Brooks Rogers, pro angler and guide

SECRET "Even if a lake has a lot of timber, the bottom contour can be important for finding fish. Look for drop-offs and other irregularities." —Brooks Rogers

SECRET "Learn to fish creek channels because bass usually are along or near them. They provide both deep water and migration routes." —Brooks Rogers

SECRET Bass will congregate at the mouths of any places into which water is being funneled, such as boat lanes through vegetation. The water

Bass will congregate wherever moving water is funneled.

might be pushed by tides, dam discharge, natural current, or even wind.

SECRET In large, shallow lakes, such as Florida's Lake Okeechobee, wind actually can produce "tides" that attract fish.

"The harder the wind, the higher the tide," says long-time Okeechobee guide and lure designer Sam Griffin. "Usually it happens in water not over 20 feet deep, and the fluctuation typically is no more than 6 inches.

"But pressure builds from the wind and creates a current that stimulates the fish."

This pressure can build not only in boat lanes, but in sloughs, between cypress trees, and along creek channels and roadbeds.

SECRET The way vegetation is leaning can tip you off to slight currents that will determine how bass are positioned. Most often, the fish will face into the current, looking for bait to come from that direction.

SECRET "Fish shallower when water is stained." —Brooks Rogers

Bass are more likely to move shallow when water is stained for the same reason that they might when the sky is cloudy or the wind is rippling the surface. Being less visible from above, they feel more secure in moving up to find a meal.

SECRET Clouds alone, however, aren't always enough to encourage bass to move shallow, especially in clear water. Sometimes they also need shadows or a breeze making chop on the surface. If the bass aren't where you thought they'd be, back off a little and fish deeper.

SECRET In summer, some bass are always in shallow water. You just have to find them. They might be under grass, or they might be around stumps and laydowns. They could be in pockets near the headwaters of a lake, where water typically is a little dingier, and flow sometimes keeps it a little cooler.

During hot August days in Alabama, George Cochran won the 1996 Bassmaster Classic by fishing a bay so shallow that his trolling motor kicked up silt. A key, he says, is whether that shallow water holds

Some bass always will hold shallow during summer. But finding them can be a challenge.

enough dissolved oxygen for the bass to be comfortable there.

SECRET Bass might be spawning in the shallows during July. But they also might be there, feeding around bluegill beds. Panfish are more likely to spawn multiple times than their larger cousins. Bass, however, aren't eating the larger spawners. Rather, they are feeding on the smaller fish that dash in to eat the eggs. To catch them, throw something that mimics a fleeing bluegill, such as a small topwater or swimbait.

SECRET Don't avoid those rough fish. Bass often are under and around schools of gar and carp.

SECRET Some of the best early season locations for smallmouth bass are shallow ledges of shale, gravel, or hard-packed sand. If drop-offs, scattered rocks, brush, or weeds are nearby, even better. Rocks add warmth to the water and attract forage such as crayfish, minnows, and insects.

"I begin fishing these areas when the water temperature is as low as 37 to 42 degrees, usually using jigs and Gitzits (tube baits). Gitzits in brown, pumpkinseed, and other dark colors seem to work best because they match the color of the crayfish," says tournament angler Lee Bailey.

SECRET "Rocks and smallmouths go hand in hand. In any lake or reservoir that has populations of walleyes and smallmouth bass, they both love rocks. Riprap, shorelines, rocky points, and rocky humps are all included. Both species inhabit these spots from late spring through

Smallmouth expert Ted Takasaki likes to look for the bronzebacks around rocks.

fall. Sometimes walleyes will take the dominant positions. But most of the time, smallmouths are the more aggressive species and will inhabit the top of the rockpile. Crayfish and other baitfish often will be on these spots. Smallies will dig into the crevasses of these rocks looking for crayfish." —Ted Takasaki, President, Lindy Little Joe tackle company

"I like to swim or barely tick the tops of these rocks for smallmouth bass with a Max Gap jig combined with a Munchies Thumpin' Grub," Takasaki adds. "Changing your speed and direction will trigger more bites. When you catch a smallie, often another will be swimming right behind. Have your partner flip another jig at that fish, and you will both catch one."

Movement

SECRET In the shallow, natural lakes of the Deep South, some bass move little from one season to the next. Their home range might be as little as a few hundred square feet. By contrast, some bass in rivers in the North migrate dozens of miles to find deepwater refuges for winter.

SECRET Many pros believe that most of our reservoirs have two distinct populations of bass. One population stays offshore except to spawn, relating more to deepwater structure and feeding primarily on shad. The other bass might migrate into deeper water during summer and winter, but prefer to feed in shallow water during spring and fall. What this means is that you can almost always find fish deep, and deep fish receive far less pressure from anglers than do those in the shallows.

SECRET "On rivers, or lakes with feeder creeks, points are good places to start hunting for largemouth and smallmouth bass. These fish will use points as transitional areas, moving into or from creeks and coves at different times during the year. Bass will find a comfort zone along the tapering flat that falls into deeper water, with brush, stumps, or some other type of cover often holding fish in these areas." —Matt Beck, tournament angler

SECRET "Late February, March, and early April are fast-action times for white bass, hybrids, and stripers, as they make their annual spawning runs up rivers and streams from reservoirs. Plastic grubs, deep crankbaits, and tailspinners are good lure choices. Bends in the channels, sandbar points, and gravel bars host large and hungry concentrations of these gamefish." —Sid Montgomery, tournament angler

SECRET "In the southern part of the country, start fishing shallow in late December." —Brooks Rogers

Many believe that bass won't move in that early, even in the South. But just a day or two of sunshine and milder temperatures will start them moving.

SECRET "As water temperatures stabilize around 60 during early spring, big female largemouths will move in to look for spawning areas. This is a good time to throw crankbaits in crayfish patterns, as well as soft plastic jerkbaits in perch color. A white spinnerbait also can be a good choice." —Lee Bailey

Bass use points as transitional areas, as they move into and out of creeks and coves.

Smell and Taste

SECRET Yes, bass are primarily sight feeders, but don't ignore the importance of other senses, especially smell, when using slow-moving soft plastic baits. If a lure looks good, but smells wrong, a bass may reject it at the last moment. Faster-moving crankbaits and spinnerbaits tend to "provoke" bass to bite, thus bypassing the importance of a bait smelling, tasting, or feeling natural.

SECRET A bass that strikes at your bait but doesn't get hooked might have missed on purpose. "When a bass bumps your grub or worm, or one rolls up on a topwater but doesn't get hooked, that fish is showing its disapproval of your lure's flavor," says Berkley fisheries scientist Keith Jones.

"Few anglers realize that fish have taste buds on their lips, on the outside of their mouths. They don't have to ingest something to determine if it's edible or a fake. Anglers always complain that they miss too many fish with topwater lures but, in fact, fish do not miss an object they want to eat," Jones adds.

SECRET Bass don't have a sweet tooth. Researchers have learned that bass reject sweet flavors instantly, and they like garlic and table salt only a little better. They prefer salt that duplicates the smell and taste of prey.

SECRET Soft plastics impregnated with or dipped in a scent *do* tend to catch more bass than those that are not. Possibly that's because the scents do attract bass. But, just as likely, scent-loaded baits also help because they mask human odor.

Wash your hands thoroughly after applying sunblock and insect repellent.

SECRET Adding a scent can provide an important edge for catching bass on soft plastics in a heavily pressured lake, and/or when they are holding tight to shallow cover, according to many of the pros. "When bass set up on stumps and other objects, that's the time to use a lot of scent," says pro Gary Klein. "When I'm fishing slowly and methodically, I can't put on enough scent. I'm a big believer."

SECRET Smoking is not just bad for your health—it also will hinder your ability to catch fish. Those nicotine-stained fingers will make your jigs and soft plastic baits less attractive to scent-sensitive bass. Also, wash your hands thoroughly after applying sunblock and insect repellent. If they get on your baits, these smells also will repel bass.

SECRET Fortunately for those of us who just can't seem to remember to wash our hands, bass are not among the fishes with the most acute sense of smell. Sharks, catfish, eels, carp, salmon, and trout all possess greater olfactory sensitivity.

Sound

SECRET Sound carries better in water than in air. That means it's all right to talk while you fish, but try to avoid banging your tackle box and other objects against the hull of your boat.

SECRET Rattles in a bait might be harmful, as well as beneficial. Many pros believe that the clearer the water, the less sound is needed as an attractant. In fact, they think that a rattling bait in clear water actually might frighten bass.

Watery World

SECRET Don't make the mistake of thinking that fish won't bite because the air temperature is below freezing. Especially early in the winter, the water temperature can be considerably warmer, and fish will be more active in their environment than you are in yours.

SECRET Colder water holds more oxygen than warm, but it also can slow down the metabolism of a cold-blooded fish and make it more inactive. That's why the slow retrieval of a suspending jerkbait can be so effective in winter. A bass has to move little to gobble up what appears to be a large, dying shad.

SECRET Fishing too deep in summer can be a waste of time. That's because our deeper lakes and reservoirs stratify as the water warms. The heavier, colder water sinks to the bottom and is separated from the upper, oxygen-rich layer by the thermocline. That middle layer prevents oxygen from reaching the depths, and therefore shad, bass, and other fish can't live there.

The depth of the thermocline will vary from one fishery to the next and mostly will depend on the nutrient load. The more fertile a lake is—because of decaying matter, fertilizer, animal wastes, and other nutrients—the more shallow the thermocline will be. In some lakes, bass might not be able to go deeper than 10 feet, even during the hottest weather.

The Bronzeback Difference

Much of the information provided in this book applies equally to largemouth and smallmouth bass. But never forget: *A smallmouth is not a largemouth*.

Stephen Headrick, a Dale Hollow Lake guide, tournament angler, and owner of Punisher Lures, credits the late Billy Westmoreland with popularizing that piece of wisdom. Westmoreland was recognized as one of the country's best smallmouth fishermen, and Headrick, who learned from Westmoreland, is no slouch. In fact, he generally is recognized as the "Smallmouth Guru."

Headrick suspects that many anglers believe that they realize that differences exist between the two species, but when it comes to actual fishing, the bronzeback gets no respect for its individuality. As a result, anglers don't catch smallmouths as readily as they might.

Here, then, is some wisdom from the Guru, to help you catch more smallmouth bass:

SECRET While largemouths generally shut off on the backside of a cold front, smallmouths can go on a feeding tear. "Smallmouth bass are built different," Headrick says. "I've seen them go crazy and just about jump into my boat after a front goes through."

SECRET Use a heavier spinnerbait for smallmouths than you would for largemouths. That's because brown bass typically hold in deeper water.

They also are more open-water oriented and likely to chase bait farther than are largemouths.

"Fishing for largemouth bass is a visual thing," Headrick says. "They are ambush predators that use grass, trees, and wood, and that's what you look for.

"With smallmouth bass, you don't need to be so visual. They use deeper water more often, and they suspend more. Find the baitfish and you will find the smallmouths."

SECRET Topwaters will catch smallmouths in open water, because they are not as cover-oriented as largemouths and because they often will suspend in and under baitfish. "The clearer the water, the faster you want to retrieve a bait like a Pop-R," the Guru explains.

SECRET A smallmouth bass will strike a plastic worm, but it much prefers a jig, which imitates one of its favorite foods, the crayfish.

"And where do smallmouths find crayfish?" Headrick asks. "They find them in rocks. You can catch smallmouths near and even in grass. We do that at Dale Hollow. But if you want to catch more smallmouths, fish jigs in rocks."

And one of the Guru's favorite jigs is a school-bus-yellow "aspirin-head" jig that he throws when the water drops below 55 degrees Fahrenheit. "Down about 15 or 20 feet, that jig looks light yellow, the same color as crayfish at that temperature," he says.

SECRET Don't wait to set the hook on a smallmouth. If you do, you'll miss the fish. "With a largemouth, you feel a tap and then wait for the second one to set the hook," Headrick says. "With a smallmouth, that first tap probably is all you are going to get. If you get a second one, you're a blessed man.

"A smallmouth is more curious than a largemouth, but it's also good at realizing if something is not good to eat."

SECRET Rattles in plastic baits probably are more beneficial for catching smallmouths than largemouths because of the brown bass's curiosity. "They're nosy as can be," the Guru says. "And that rattle draws their attention.

"I've dived in Dale Hollow to study the bass. If you rattle the grass, a smallmouth will come to look. A largemouth swims away."

SECRET If you are looking for spawning smallmouths, don't go back into pockets. Largemouths might build their nests there, but not the bronzebacks. Instead, focus on flats in 8 to 15 feet of water. "Smallmouths like to feed on windblown flats," Headrick says. "But they like their spawning areas to be a little more protected."

Angler Behavior

SECRET If you want to be a better angler, don't just study bass behavior. Study your own. Make certain that everything that you do when on the water helps, rather than hinders.

Time and again, for example, I've seen an angler who is striking out refuse to switch to a bait like the one that his partner is using to catch fish. "Here," his friend will say. "Try one of these."

"No, thanks," says the luckless fisherman. "I'll just stick with this."

That's just plain dumb. You have to throw a bait that the fish is willing to eat, not a bait that you want it to eat. And what's your priority? Defending your ego or catching fish? Mine is catching fish.

SECRET When you share a boat or shoreline with someone who seems to be a better angler than you, watch his behavior as well. Learn from him by paying attention to all the little things that he does, especially if you are both using the same bait and he is catching more fish.

How is he holding his rod? Is it higher or lower than yours? Is his retrieve steady or erratic? Are you retrieving as slowly or quickly as he is?

Also, are you using the same kind of reel that he is? That can make a big difference. Different brands of reels retrieve line at different rates, depending on the gear ratio. Some are 6.2:1. Others are 5:1 or even slower.

The higher the first number, the more line is retrieved with each turn of the reel handle. That makes it a "faster" reel. You can slow down with a fast reel, but it's really tough to speed up with a "slow" reel. So if your angling partner is using a faster or slower reel than you are, that could make a difference.

If the fishing is tough for both of you, here are some angler behavior strategies that might work for you: Slow down your retrieve, especially if you're fishing a worm or other soft plastic. Use a smaller bait. When fish aren't aggressive, they sometimes prefer smaller prey. Use a different color bait. Shades (dark, light) usually are more important than specific colors. But if fishing is tough, a slight variation can make a difference.

SECRET The pros almost universally agree that concentration is a key to catching bass. If the bite is slow, a good way to maintain concentration is to fish one of your confidence baits. Another good way is to keep telling yourself that a bite will come on the next cast, and you must be prepared for it.

SECRET When you are catching fish, always think in terms of identifying a pattern. How deep are the fish? Which side of the stumps are they holding on? How fast is my retrieve? And don't stop there. As long as the bite persists, keep refining that pattern.

"You want to refine it to where you can make a run down a lake and say, 'This is the right stuff,' pull in, and catch them there also," says pro Shaw Grigsby. "The more you can refine it, the more you can repeat it, and that's the biggest thing."

SECRET Practice, practice, practice. Casting ability is one of the main reasons that the pros are better than the rest of us. More often than not, a pro can drop his bait exactly where he wants it to go, an important consideration when bass are holding tight to cover and the difference between success and failure is a matter of inches.

SECRET Just as important as the ability to put the bait where you want it is the ability to do so in an unobtrusive manner, especially when bass are shallow. A bait that splashes like a rock being thrown into the water likely will scare the fish that you are trying to catch. But a bait that enters the water softly will tend to arouse its curiosity and make it more susceptible to being caught. Underhand and sidearm casts typically provide the quietest presentations.

SECRET If you hire a guide, listen to him! Use the baits that he recommends and throw to the places that he suggests—at least for a while. You might learn something, and you might catch some fish.

Once while I was fishing with a particularly hardheaded friend, our guide pointed and told my partner to cast there. He refused, preferring to focus on what he thought was a better spot. I threw where the guide suggested and caught a 9-pound bass.

SECRET Keep a diary. Or a journal. Or a log. Whatever you want to call it, keep a record of how, when, and where you catch bass. Many of the pros do. Some also keep computerized data of each lake that they fish, detailing time, season, conditions, and methods that they used to catch bass there. They use that information not only to help them learn about specific lakes, but to identify baits, tactics, and patterns that might work in similar fisheries in other places.

Practice casting. The pros are better than the rest of us because they do it so much.

3

Weather

Weather influences fish behavior. Probably every angler can remember times when fish turned on or off because of a change in the weather. But science and myth mix freely when anglers try to understand and explain why fish behavior alters because of high pressure, low pressure, wind, and other weather variables. The following should help you better understand why and how bass really are affected and, as a result, just could help make you a better angler.

Barometric Pressure

Generally moving from west to east, areas of high and low pressure determine our weather.

As high pressure moves in, winds tend to blow clockwise and away from the center. Weather within the center of a high-pressure area features clear skies, dry air, little or no wind, and cooler temperatures. Especially during fall and winter, high pressure brings sunny, bluebird skies, cold winds, and poor fishing.

With the approach of a low-pressure area, the wind blows counterclockwise and toward the center. Weather within the center of a low-pressure area features cloudy skies, high humidity, light winds, steadier temperatures, and possibly precipitation. Fishing almost always is better under these conditions.

Changes occur as one type of pressure is pushed out by another. A low-pressure area moving in typically brings unstable weather and falling barometric pressure. Falling pressure, anglers know, typically coincides with better fishing.

But maybe not for the reason that many believe. Some think that high pressure makes fish uncomfortable, which is why they don't bite well upon the arrival of fair weather and a rising barometer. They also believe that falling pressure prompts fish to become more active.

Weather influences bass behavior, but myth mixes freely with fact in trying to figure out how.

Actually, what probably happens is that falling pressure allows plankton and tiny invertebrates to become more buoyant and float upward. This makes them easier prey for shad and minnows. The increased activity of these forage species, in turn, triggers bass and other gamefish to feed.

Or falling pressure simply might be an indicator of more favorable conditions overall, according to Bob Ponds, a former professional angler who worked as a radar specialist and supervisor for the U.S. Air Force and the National Weather Service.

"If you have falling pressure, you're going to have high humidity and clouds. It will be darker, and the fish will stray out farther from where they have been hiding and they will bite better," he says. "Barometric pressure doesn't affect how fish bite so much as it indicates conditions that affect how they will bite."

And what happens when the barometer rises? Why do the fish stop biting? Here's one theory:

Especially during fall and winter, high pressure can bring sunny skies, cold winds, and poor fishing.

"When you've got a rising barometer, fish are going to seek eddies and structure to take the pressure off them," says Sam Griffin, a lure maker and guide on Florida's Lake Okeechobee. "We can feel a temperature change. They can feel a pressure change. We think that fish hide in cover and behind structure to feed. They also do it to rest."

SECRET Changing atmospheric pressure is not as likely to affect fish behavior in rivers and streams as it is in lakes and impoundments. That's because water flow in these fisheries is a more dominant factor for increasing or decreasing pressure than is the air.

Temperature

Water is slower to heat and cool than air. What this means is that anglers shouldn't be too concerned about brief warm or cold spells. Rather, they should watch and react to long-term trends, just as the fish do. Slowly warming temperatures in the spring prompt fish to start to move shallow, feed, and prepare for reproduction. Cooling water in the fall triggers them to follow bait and fatten up, before moving deep for winter.

For better success, anglers should key into these seasonal patterns, but also remember that timing can vary from a few days to a few weeks, depending on the severity of a season's weather.

"Trends mean more than anything," Ponds says. "If the water is 50 degrees, the fish may or may not bite. If the temperature is going up, it likely will turn fish on. If it's cooling, then you'll probably have a tougher time."

SECRET During winter, anglers also should remember that every rule has an exception, and just a few hours' worth of sun can make a difference. It can warm a shallow cove, especially if it is on the north end of a lake, where it catches the heat from the sun in the southern sky, and that warmth can activate invertebrates and forage species, which, in turn, attract gamefish. Rocks and/or a dark bottom also can absorb heat and warm the water, triggering the same phenomenon.

In addition, the northern shallows of a lake will warm faster overall than the other areas. In the spring this means an earlier bite than in the rest of the lake.

Wind

Most anglers believe that fishing is best with a west wind and worst with an east wind. They are partially correct.

Good fishing can seem to arrive with a west wind, because wind from the west or southwest often indicates that a low-pressure front is approaching—and with it a falling barometer. In this case, wind direction is not a factor in determining how cooperative the fish will be, but rather an indicator of a positive factor.

But if the low-pressure area is far enough to the southwest, the wind will be from the east, and barometric pressure still will fall, an indicator that the fishing is about to improve.

SECRET Actually, a south wind is the most reliable as an indicator of good fishing. It could mean that low pressure is moving in from the west, or that high pressure is moving away to the east.

A breeze from the west probably is second best, with east ranking third, and north the least favorable for fishing.

But there are exceptions.

"When it's cold, you have weeds, and there's a north wind, the bigger the wind the better," says Norm Klayman, a tournament angler and longtime guide on Bull Shoals Lake. "The fish in the weeds go crazy over a fast-moving crankbait. I've seen it time after time at Lake Fork and at Lake Guerrero in Mexico."

Besides being an indicator of barometric pressure, wind can affect fishing in another way, as it creates currents and makes waves. These push plankton and zooplankton forward until they strike a windblown shore and then accumulate. Shad and other forage species move in to feed on these invertebrates, and the gamefish follow.

SECRET If the wind is blowing along a shoreline, instead of directly at it, eddies can form on the sheltered sides of points. Bass and other predators often will frequent these calmer waters, waiting for the food to come to them.

Wind also can work in an angler's favor by reducing light penetration and distorting the light that does penetrate, so that the fish sees no clear image of anything above. This could translate into an all-day bite on topwater baits or shallow-running baits, even if the sun is shining. On the negative side, fish are more likely to miss what they strike at, if they can't see as well.

SECRET This wind-related information won't help you catch bass. But it might help you deal with the frustration that you feel after the weatherman (or woman) predicted winds of 10 to 15 miles per hour for your fishing trip—and you were blown off the water by a gale. To get a more accurate idea of how hard the wind is going to blow, take those two numbers and add them together. So, if the meteorologist says 5 to

Don't wait until a storm is near to make your run to a marina.

10, you will know that the wind likely will be closer to 15. And if he says 15 to 20, you just might want to stay home—or go fly a kite.

Oh, yes, when this formula proves inaccurate, it's almost always because the total is on the low side of the actual wind speed. You have been warned.

Humidity

Humidity itself doesn't affect the behavior of fish, since they live in a liquid environment. But anglers should remember that rising humidity indicates the approach of a low-pressure system—and falling barometric pressure.

Precipitation

As with humidity, falling rain or snow has little effect on how comfortable fish are in their environment and, consequently, on how actively they will feed.

Precipitation, however, can have an effect through the runoff that it creates. Cold and/or muddy water pouring into the back of a cove typically will drive fish away.

SECRET But runoff from a rain that is warmer than the lake can draw fish like a magnet, especially in early spring or late fall.

Lightning

Get off the water when you see a storm with lightning approaching. Fish don't like lightning any more than we do. Crackles and booms disrupt their environment and send them scurrying for cover.

SECRET "Never wait until a storm is near to make your run in to the marina. Most lightning is found on the leading edge of a front, and your chances of being struck are higher if you run just in front of the storm. Your odds are much better if you leave well in advance or sit tight and wait for it to pass. Summer thunderstorms last only an average of 20 minutes. So if in doubt, wait it out." —Kathy Magers, pro angler

Fog

Don't be fooled by fog. Yes, it does block the sun, which would seem to contribute to better fishing. Actually, though, fog usually indicates that a cold, high-pressure system has settled over a layer of warmer air. In other words, the barometer is rising, which turns off the bite.

Sun

Sun is the power cell for fueling our fisheries. It enhances the growth of plants, which, in turn, provide oxygen for fish and other aquatic species.

Fog more often is a sign of poor fishing conditions than good.

When water is too rich in nutrients—usually from pollution—the sun can trigger massive algae blooms, which prevent light from reaching beneficial vegetation. Also, the algae often die when they don't receive sunlight for several days. Their decay then sucks oxygen out of the water, possibly causing fish kills.

Environmental considerations aside, the brighter the sun, the greater the light penetration into water and the greater depths at which fish can see and plants can grow.

On sunny days, bass are more likely to be shallow at dawn and dusk.

SECRET On sunny days, look for fish on the deep sides of grass beds. At dawn and dusk and on cloudy days, look for them to be more shallow.

Moon

Many bass anglers will tell you that fish bite better at night just before, during, and just after a full moon. Others like the new moon. Little evidence, however, supports the notion that bass eat more at night during certain phases of the moon.

Little evidence, that is, except angler success. And who's to argue with that?

"It's definitely not a coincidence that a lot of big fish are caught three days before and after a full moon," says C. B. Bowlin, an Illinois guide and tournament fisherman.

SECRET Just before, during, and after a full moon, you're more likely to catch bass, especially largemouths, by fishing from dusk until midnight, when the moon is high. With a new moon, your best bet will be from midnight until dawn.

Still, the fact remains that bass don't see well at night, even under a full moon in a clear sky. If they are biting better during this time, perhaps it is because insects, at the base of the food chain, are more active and this, in turn, triggers heightened activity all the way up to the top predators.

"It's my gut feeling that changes in the weather, whether temperature, pressure, day length, or light, may be affecting lower things on the food chain. These are things we can't measure, but they have a profound influence on bass behavior," says Gene Gilliland, a fisheries biologist and tournament angler.

Put some clouds over a full moon, though, and you darken the theory that more insect activity is occurring because of increased light. On the other hand, if the water is clear, it makes sense that aquatic life will be more active than it would be in murky water, because moonlight can penetrate better—even when filtered by clouds. Perhaps that is why night fishing is most popular on clearwater impoundments.

In salt water, no question exists that the moon affects when and how well fish will bite. That's because the moon determines the length and strength of tides, and this tidal flow turns fish on and off. Typically, fish bite better on incoming tides, as they wash in food and allow predators to move into previously inaccessible shallows. But high tides also can provide good fishing in some waters, as can outgoing tides. Outgoing tides, though, will send fish in the other direction, and anglers must act accordingly if they want to catch them.

Conclusion

"I don't look at the barometric pressure, and I don't look at the moon phases," says Ponds. "I look at the sky.

"Winds and clouds are the keys. Temperature trends are important, too, and they are affected by those same winds and clouds."

More Weather Secrets

SECRET Most of the time, a weather front will impact you before it does the fish. Don't make the mistake of thinking that bass instantly shut off when the wind shifts from south to north and you hurry to put on a jacket. Water changes more slowly than air, and consequently, so do its inhabitants.

SECRET Florida does get cold. If you're going to the Sunshine State for a winter fishing trip, take warm clothing. And take some jigs and soft plastics for flipping and pitching. During the cold snap, those Florida bass will hold tight to cover.

SECRET Sometimes a cold front is good.

Florida does get cold, as is evident on this frigid day near Orlando.

"In the middle of fall, the worst thing that can happen is a really bad hot spell," says former Bassmaster Classic champion Mark Davis. "A cool spell in the fall makes the shad bunch up and makes the locations of bass much more predictable."

SECRET Wind can create fish-holding currents, especially on lakes and impoundments covered with aquatic vegetation. Keep an eye on floating leaves and debris to find the currents.

SECRET When you follow a high tide up a coastal river, keep a close eye on the falling tide to avoid getting stranded.

Not that something good couldn't happen from getting stranded. Christiana Bradley, a Women's Bassmaster Tour competitor, spent her first date with her future husband immobilized in the Rappahannock River.

"We went out on Father's Day," she says. "We got the boat stuck on a flat in the river and had to wait—not only for the tide to come back in, but we had to wait for it to finish going out and then come back in. What a day!

"There was little said for the first couple of hours," she continues. "Then I called my sister and asked her to rent a helicopter and have it drop a six-pack to us. He finally laughed and we eventually decided we would go have a steak dinner after we got the boat out. Neither one of us complained. It was like we were where we wanted to be, finally spending time with each other.

"Several months later, he asked me to marry him while we were flipping lily pads in a creek."

So . . . if you are fishing a tidal river and even the least bit fearful of getting stuck, take a date and a six-pack.

SECRET A hard wind blowing into a river can make a high tide even higher. And a wind blowing out on a low tide can turn shallows into dry land.

SECRET As winter turns to spring, the north end of a lake will warm fastest. Therefore, that is the first place to look for fish moving shallow.

SECRET "Follow the shade line as the sun moves throughout the day. Fish often will remain active along it." —Rick Lillegard

SECRET Some dedicated smallmouth anglers will fish only a shaded bank under a full moon. While some light is good, they believe that the fish are just as turned off by bright moonlight as they are by sunlight.

SECRET Others believe that success at night is tied less to phases of the moon and more to the fact that water skiers and personal watercraft aren't out churning up the water after dark.

SECRET Crayfish, a smallmouth favorite, are nocturnal, which helps get bronzebacks up and moving after dark.

4

Tackle and Equipment

Professional anglers view their rods, reels, electronics, boats, and other equipment as the tools of their trade, as their means of making a living. Consequently, they take good care of them. And they work diligently to learn how to get the most out of each and every "tool." You should too.

Boat and Tow Vehicle

SECRET Keep an extra key for your vehicle hidden somewhere in your boat. You'll be glad you did when you accidentally drop your key ring into the water as you're getting into or out of your boat.

Keep an extra key for your vehicle hidden somewhere in your boat.

SECRET "Always carry tire plugs and cans of air and pliers. When you get a flat, find the object embedded in your tire, pull it out with the pliers, insert the plug, and refill the tire with air cans. This saves you the time and effort required to jack up the vehicle and put the spare on. Using plugs, you can have your rig back on the road in less than 10 minutes." —Lance Vick, pro angler

SECRET When trying to pass a semi, wait until you are approaching an uphill climb, where his load most likely will slow him down. Trying to pass on a downhill slope will cause both vehicles to pick up speed, making it more dangerous.

"A speeding ticket taught me this lesson," says pro Kathy Magers.

SECRET "When hitching the boat trailer to the tow vehicle, if it sticks and the coupler will not fall down onto the ball, keep your cool. Rather than banging on it or jumping up and down on the bumper, pull the trailer forward or backward an inch. Usually, being in a bind with too much pressure causes it to stick." —Kathy Magers

SECRET "Crisscross the left and right trailer chain hooks before attaching to your tow vehicle, making a "cradle" for the trailer tongue to fall into should it uncouple. This prevents the trailer tongue from dragging on the pavement and potentially flipping your rig." —Kathy Magers

SECRET "When launching the boat by yourself, tie a rope that's at least 20 feet long to your tow bar, where the hooks from the trailer go, and tie the other end to the eye on the bow of the boat. Then slowly back the boat down until it just starts to slide back. This also is helpful in rough weather." —Christiana Bradley, pro angler

SECRET "Inspect your boat prior to launching. Check such things as the props, drain plug, oil, and fuel bulb." —Rick Lillegard

SECRET On your transom saver, take a hammer and pound closed the safety strap so it won't come off.

"I do only one end, the end opposite the side of the motor with the trim switch," says guide Steve Chaconas. "I also always have the transom saver with the nut side down on the bolt that allows you to adjust the length of the saver. This is just in case the nut comes off. Gravity will keep the bolt in place to avoid losing the entire setup."

SECRET "Buy quality electronics and learn how to use them." —Brooks Rogers

SECRET "Use variable speed control for appropriate thrust with your trolling motor and avoid using the on/off switch." —Rick Lillegard

SECRET When you take passengers, go over the safety check, telling them where to find the personal floatation devices (PFDs), throwable device, and fire extinguisher.

"I also show them how to board the boat—from the back—if they fall overboard," says Chaconas. "And this is the time when I tell them the windshield is not a handle! If they break it, they buy it. I point out that there is a step to the back deck and it is not the seat."

Hooks

SECRET "Most anglers who use jigs know that bass and wood cover go together like cornbread and buttermilk. They also know that hang-ups in heavy cover are common. A few seconds to check the integrity of the jig's hook after such a hang-up will help ensure that you catch the next fish that bites." —Matt Beck

SECRET "When fishing crankbaits around rocks, make frequent checks of the treble hooks. The hook points can become damaged or dulled, especially the front hooks." —Tim Horton, pro angler

Make frequent checks of the treble hooks when fishing crankbaits around rocks.

SECRET "Always use premium hooks, and change the hooks on your baits after you've used them awhile or if they were hung often in heavy cover. The extra money that you spend will be a small price to pay when you hook the fish of a lifetime." —Lance Vick

SECRET When fishing soft plastics, don't use just any old long-shank hook that you find lying in your tackle box. Different styles and sizes of baits require different styles and sizes of hooks. On a thick-bodied bait, for example, you want a wide-gap hook that will cut through the bait and stick a bass when you set the hook.

SECRET Red hooks work. I'm not saying that more bass automatically will bite your baits if you use red hooks. This is where the confidence factor enters the angling equation. I believe that a splash of red on a bait makes it more attractive to predatory fish. Red, after all, is the color of blood, as well as gills. So when I use red hooks, I'm a more confident—and consequently better—angler. What I don't like about red hooks is that the coating wears off quickly.

Line

Dave Burkhardt, owner of Triple Fish International (TFI), is one of the most knowledgeable people in the angling industry regarding fishing lines. He's also one of the best anglers I know, with two 15-pound bass to his credit, as well as a 14, a 13-8, and a host of additional double-digit fish.

His favorite line? Fluorocarbon.

"The cat's out of the bag now," says Burkhardt, whose line company is based in Clermont, Florida. "Probably half the guys (pros) are throwing it now, and fluorocarbon is the fastest-growing line category."

Before his company came up with affordable filler spools, fluorocarbon was used solely as leader material, mostly by saltwater anglers.

"There's still a big disparity in brands," he adds. "But they're all improving. And now a 200-yard spool is about $10. That's no more than copolymer line and about half the cost of braid. Fluorocarbon for leader used to be $1 a foot."

Why should you be throwing fluorocarbon line, on at least some of your reels?

SECRET Because of light refraction, fluorocarbon virtually disappears in water, meaning that you can use a stronger test—10-pound instead of 8, for example—and consequently, you are less likely to have a bass break off.

Fluorocarbon has 20 percent less stretch and 1.8 times more density than monofilament. That translates into a more sensitive line, meaning you can feel bites easier. Less stretch also means that you can make longer casts and still have an effective hookset.

Because it's heavier, fluorocarbon will get a sinking bait into the strike zone faster. And if you are fishing a weightless soft bait, it will keep you in closer contact with the bait as it falls.

Finally, it's more resistant to ultraviolet rays, meaning you don't have to replace it on your reel as often, and it's more abrasion-resistant than monofilament.

The negative: Because fluorocarbon is heavier than monofilament, it will impede the action of a topwater bait. And it's not a good choice for fishing a soft plastic over grass, since it will drag down and tangle the bait.

"I now use fluorocarbon about 75 percent of the time," says Cliff Pace, a Mississippi pro who is sponsored by Hi-Seas fishing line. "When it first came out, I used it only about 20 percent of the time. About the only times that I don't use it now are when I'm casting a topwater or when I'm flipping heavy vegetation and prefer to go with braid."

Braided line's primary advantages are its lack of stretch and its durability, Burkhardt says.

SECRET Because of the difference in stretch, an angler should not set a hook with the same force using braid as he would using fluorocarbon and, especially, monofilament, which can stretch by 25 percent or more. A hard hookset with braid can break a rod or straighten a hook. A good way to adjust the strength of the hookset is by tightening or loosening the drag.

Braid's negatives are its higher cost, its greater visibility (not so important when flipping), and its weaker knot strength.

Monofilament, meanwhile, is a very forgiving line because of its stretch.

SECRET But mono also becomes weaker as it is stretched. That's one of the main reasons that pros change the line on their reels so often.

Copolymer, the fourth and final category of line, is a more sophisticated product, and therefore generally costs more. "The mix of characteristics can make it more durable and softer," Burkhardt says.

SECRET Copolymer typically has a 20 percent smaller diameter than mono. That means you can get greater strength by using a higher-test line, without impeding the performance of a bait.

That smaller diameter also means that you can spool more line on your reel. And being softer than mono, it will lie better on the spool, with less looping and coiling.

"There are so many kinds of line out there that choosing what to use can be confusing," Burkhardt says. "But each of the four kinds is a tool for specific jobs. You can put braid on all of your reels to save money and have stout line, but that doesn't mean you will catch more fish."

SECRET The San Diego knot, also known as the reverse clinch knot, is Pace's choice for use with fluorocarbon line. "The Palomar breaks at a lower knot strength than the San Diego," he says.

Here's how to tie the San Diego:

First, pass the line through the eye of the hook, bait, or swivel. Then double back over the main line.

Next, make turns over the main line. The number of turns will vary with the strength of the line, with fewer needed for higher tests. Use eight turns for 10-pound line and three for 40.

Run the tag end of the line through the loop of line at the eye. Holding the coils in place, push the tag end through the turn at the top of the knot.

Holding the tag and the main line, pull on the coils. They should be in a spiral and not overlap. Trim the tag end.

As you might suspect, the knot first was popularized in San Diego, where anglers go out on long-range boats to chase tuna. It might seem a little complicated at first, but the tuna anglers learned that they could tie it quickly once they'd had a little practice. It's also becoming a popular knot for braided lines.

SECRET "Lighter line will give a lure more action, while heavier line will do the opposite. Experiment and let the fish's response determine what type of action that it prefers." —Zell Rowland, pro angler

SECRET "Freshwater anglers can save money on line by using backing on their reels. By placing about 25 to 30 yards of 20-pound line onto the core of the spool and then attaching the appropriate fishing line to the backing and filling the spool, an angler can save a considerable amount of money over the year." —Matt Beck

SECRET "You can save time, line, and money when you respool your reel. Don't strip off all the line. Instead, cut off the length of about 1½ casts. Then tie new line to the old with a blood knot and fill the reel." —Lance Vick

SECRET Take advantage of technology when respooling your reels.

"I thought every tournament angler used this tool, the Berkley Line Spooling Station," says Christiana Bradley. "But the more pros I meet, the more I see that's not true. I am spoiled with this thing now. If the batteries go dead on the line stripper, I will go get new batteries before stripping my reels by hand.

"In addition to the convenience and speed, the spooling station keeps steady pressure on the line and prevents me from having to sit on the floor with a spool of line and a pencil between my feet."

SECRET "When using a braided line, apply glue to the knot to maximize its strength." —Dave Burkhardt

SECRET "Leave a little monofilament backing on your reel and tie it to the braided line before spooling with the braided. Or use electrical tape to secure the braided line to the reel spool. If you tie braided line directly to the spool, it will slide and your drag won't work properly." —Dave Burkhardt

SECRET "Twist line around rods for storage. To do this, grab line in the center and then spin the rod." —Rick Lillegard

SECRET "When retying a bait, strip line to the dent formed in the line by the rod tip when you hook your lure to the reel or hook keeper." —Rick Lillegard

SECRET "Use fluorocarbon to get deeper with your crankbaits. The smaller diameter and greater density of the line allows you to get 15 percent deeper than with most monofilaments of equivalent strength." —Dave Burkhardt

SECRET "In clear water, lighter line almost always is better." —Brooks Rogers

SECRET Sunshine and heat will deteriorate many fishing lines, especially those made of monofilament. Protect them when possible.

SECRET Run hot water on the spool of your spinning reel to remove line memory.

SECRET Use a fluorescent line for night fishing, especially if you are fishing with jigs or soft plastics for smallmouth bass. Bites on slow-moving baits tend to be more subtle at night, and if you are using fluorescent line with a blacklight, you just might see what you didn't feel.

SECRET Be extra wary about using braided line in Florida—or anywhere else alligators live. Gators will strike artificial baits, and foul-hooking one always is a possibility. If you hang one with braided line, you will not be able to break it off. As long as you have a pair of scissors or a knife, that might not pose a problem. But if you are unprepared . . .

Outside the (Tackle) Box

SECRET No pro goes on the water without a lure retriever. Some simply close the gap on a spark plug, snap on a swivel, and let it slide down the line. Others attach commercially made lure knockers to rope, retractable dog leashes, or strong braided line on an old casting reel.

No pro goes on the water without a lure retriever.

SECRET A chain stringer with a 2-ounce weight attached makes a good retriever for rods and reels, according to pro Emily Shaffer. Just open all the metal keepers, attach it to a rope, and drag the bottom.

SECRET If you are going to run your boat through lots of aquatic plants, take along a toilet bowl brush, says Matt Beck of Florida.

"My engine's vents can easily get clogged with muck, hydrilla, or other vegetation. While idling through cover, I keep a sharp eye on my water pressure gauge, and when it starts to drop, I immediately shut down the engine before it overheats."

He then trims it out of the water and uses the brush to clear the water intake vents. "Not only will this save you time at the end of the day by not having to wait for your engine to cool down, it will save the life of your engine by preventing damage due to overheating," he adds.

SECRET Take along a saw if you fish backwaters. Pro Penny Berryman learned that the hard way after trying to back out of a slough, past a large, low-hanging limb. "The next thing I knew, I was pinned to the front deck, stuck with a mossy, dirty, heavy limb sliming me from one end to the other," she says. "The saw has come in handy several times since then."

SECRET Use finishing nails to add weight to Senkos and soft jerk-baits when you need them to fall faster.

"If I run out of nails and am not able to get to a store to buy more, I take a metal clothes hanger and cut off lengths to use," says pro Judy Wong.

SECRET With a cigar tube and a small rubber band, you can keep your plastic worm or lizard from sliding down the shank on a Texas rig.

Put the band on the neck of the tube and double it. Put the soft plastic in the tube and then slide the band onto the neck of the bait.

SECRET A large tumbler glass helps pro Kathy Magers add scent to her soft plastics. She pours it about ¼ inch deep into the glass.

"Then I cautiously prop it in a corner of my front storage box. After rigging, I simply open the lid and dunk the lure, rather than spraying scent, which wind carries and is bad for carpets," she says.

SECRET Or try Preparation H as a fish attractant. That's what pro angler Dianna Clark uses. "It has shark liver oil in it," she says. "I don't know if that's why it works. But it does."

SECRET "Duco Cement, a multipurpose household glue, is good for sealing topwater baits. It takes about 10 minutes to dry." —Sam Griffin

SECRET String your worm hooks on safety pins, sorted by size. That way, you can more quickly and easily find the size you want.

SECRET When you travel, take along some duct tape. Place some strips on your rod tube or wrap some around an ink pen or marker.

Instead of spraying—and wasting—scent, keep some in a tumbler glass and dip your baits into it.

Among its many uses, the tape can be used to patch holes in luggage and tackle bags, secure a rod to a reel, and temporarily hold rod eyes in place. My rod tube is telescoping, so I also use the tape to firm up the joint in the middle. I learned to do this after an airline loosened the joint and turned all of my 6-6 rods into 6-footers.

SECRET A small ice chest makes an excellent dry storage container for clothes and camera gear.

SECRET If you regularly have to carry your rods and tackle a long way to your boat, or if you fish from a pier or the bank, an old golf bag is a good way to lighten your load. Just put it on a roller cart, load it up, and pull it with you.

Reels

SECRET Good maintenance advice to remember is to grease the gears and oil the bearings. But too much oil can be just as bad as too little. Too much will make the bearings sluggish. Just a drop is best.

Also, avoid using aerosols. Sprayed-on oil is more likely to leave a messy film and more likely to evaporate, leaving no lubricant.

Here are some general maintenance tips for levelwind reels from Lake Fork Tackle Repair:

Outside of reel: Wipe the entire reel to remove dirt, salt, and crud. Use a cotton swab to reach into tight places.

Hub or brake drum: Use a cotton swab and alcohol to clean the brake hub or brake drum, as well as the spool edge. Then apply a small bit of oil to the inside of the hub or drum.

Spool shaft: Clean in similar fashion to that used for hub. Apply drop of oil to ends of shaft.

Bearings: If the bearings are dirty, clean and apply a drop of oil. If they are not dirty, simply add oil.

Cast control cap: Remove cap inner parts and clean with cotton swab. If copper part is dented, turn it over and apply one drop of oil.

Levelwind or worm gear: Clean with a swab or pipe cleaner. Add a drop of oil on each end.

Handle knobs: Apply one drop of oil.

SECRET Lighten up on both your drag and your hookset if you have put braided line on your baitcasting reel. Braided line typically is much stronger than monofilament and has less stretch. If you don't adjust accordingly, you could rip a hook right through the mouth of a big fish or tear a large hole that allows the hook to fall out.

SECRET "After making the first cast of the morning, be sure to "break" your drag free by pulling a few inches of line from the spool. This will ensure that the drag system is in proper working order when it is needed. The drag system of a reel can stick after sitting for a few days, and that extra tension on the line during a fight might be all that's needed for your line to break when you are battling a big fish." —Matt Beck

SECRET When you're not going to use a reel for several days or more, loosen the drag. That will help extend the life of the reel and keep the drag working smoothly. Don't forget to tighten it back up when you go fishing.

SECRET Keep the spool full on your baitcasting reel if you want to get maximum performance. A full spool will allow the reel to retrieve the maximum amount of line on each revolution. An almost empty spool will take in much less line with each turn.

SECRET Know the gear ratios of your baitcasting reels. A "fast" reel, such as 7:1, will retrieve more line with each turn of the handle than will a "slow" reel, such as 5:1. If you don't know your gear ratios, you might

Make sure that your drag is working properly or you could lose a bass at the boat.

think that you are fishing a bait as slowly as your partner, who is catching all the fish. But likely you're not. The gear ratio is printed on the box and stamped or engraved on the reel, as well as explained in the instruction manual.

SECRET If you're fishing with a crankbait, you might think that you want a faster reel, but probably you don't. That's because fast reels are used mostly when fishing soft plastics, to take up slack line quickly before the hookset or to get the bait back to the boat in a hurry after it is out of the strike zone.

Slower reels usually—although not always—are better for fast-moving crankbaits. For one thing, they allow time for the baits to reach their proper depths. For another, they allow for more erratic, lifelike action.

SECRET If you use round baitcasting reels and your hands are really achy or tired at the end of the day, you might want to switch to "low-profile" reels. They're much easier to hold, and therefore less painful to use, especially if you have small hands.

SECRET A spinning reel does have its place in a bass boat. You can better skip a bait under a dock with a spinning reel than with a baitcaster. You can more easily drop a bait vertically. You can more carefully present light baits in shallow water, where the bass are wary. Yet many

A spinning reel does have its place in a bass boat.

anglers refuse to use them, thus denying themselves a valuable tool in their quest to catch bass. Look in the rod storage locker of almost any pro, and you'll see several spinning reels.

SECRET When fishing with a spinning reel, flip the bail closed with your free hand and you will avoid line twist and troublesome loops. Giving the line a slight tug before closing the bail also will help, especially if the line is 6-pound test or lighter.

Rods

SECRET "Always control your rod position to be ready for a hookset."
—Rick Lillegard

SECRET One of the most common rod-related problems occurs when you attach the lure to the handle and then reel the line too tight for temporary storage. Over time, this will pit and break the ceramic guide at the end of the rod.

SECRET Watch out for those rod tips when you walk into your accommodations at a fishing camp in the tropics. Almost all of these places have ceiling fans that will whack the end off a rod if you're not careful.

SECRET One rod is not enough. Every professional bass angler typically has a half dozen or more types of rods in the boat, each with a specific application. One will be a long, stiff rod for flipping. That enables the angler to yank a bass quickly out of heavy cover.

Pros will have a rod with backbone but a sensitive tip for fishing Texas-rig soft plastics. That allows them to feel even the slightest bite and drive home the hook.

They will also have a "soft" graphite or fiberglass rod for fishing crankbaits and/or topwaters. That flexibility allows a bass to shake its head and still not tear loose from the treble hooks, as it might with a stiffer, unforgiving rod.

A pro also might carry different rods for Carolina rigs, jigs, suspending jerkbaits, spinnerbaits, and finesse baits. If you can't afford such luxury, at least go with a stiffer rod with sensitive tip for soft plastics, jigs, and spinnerbaits, and a more flexible rod for baits with treble hooks.

SECRET When you buy a rod, know what you're getting. If you purchase a crankbait rod to fish soft plastics, you're going to lose fish with it.

A graphite rod typically is labeled with "weight" (heavy, medium, or light) and "action." The first doesn't refer to how much a rod weighs, but rather how much force is required to bend it. A heavy rod allows an angler to generate powerful hooksets and work a fish to the boat quickly.

One rod is not enough. A long, stiff rod is best for flipping, but a poor choice for throwing a crankbait.

With its greater flexibility, a medium or light rod allows an angler to guide a crankbait more easily. Also, its easier bend doesn't provide leverage for a fish to tear out treble hooks from its jaw as it jumps, twists, and shakes its head.

"Action" refers to the bend of the rod. Fast-action rods bend mostly in the tip, while those with slower actions bend more throughout the rod's length. The faster the action, the better the rod at long and accurate casts and the quicker it straightens back out. A fast and flexible tip also helps an angler detect bites on soft plastics. But because it straightens back out so quickly, a fast-action rod is not a good choice for crankbaits, for the same reason a heavy rod is not.

By the way, you'll have to look long and hard to find a rod tip that doesn't contain "fast" in its description. The slowest generally are rated "moderate fast," while the fastest are "extra fast."

Oh, yes, why is it not a good idea to fish a worm with a crankbait rod? The "softer" rod makes it more difficult for an angler to drive home the hook through a plastic bait. Thus, a bass is more likely to avoid being stuck and, if hooked, is more likely to escape during the fight.

SECRET Rods also carry recommended line and lure weight ratings. You're more likely to break a rod if you use a line or lure heavier than what it's designed to handle.

SECRET Don't determine what length rod to use by how tall or short you are, says pro angler Kathy Magers.

"A rod's length is what takes out slack and sets the hook. It's all about leverage," she adds. "So regardless of your size or gender, the rod length needs to match the task at hand. What might need shortening on women's rods is the handle—the butt of the rod—since many women hold the rod in front of them while fishing.

"I've always cut off about 2 inches of my cork handles so that they don't bump my ribs or hips while I'm casting or working topwater lures. One word of caution: Be sure expandable rods are fully extended before cutting or you'll end up with a 3-piece rod that won't stay together."

SECRET Quality matters. My friend who used G.Loomis rods used to consistently outfish me when we threw soft plastics and jigs. Once I made the switch, the odds evened out. The difference in "feel" between a quality rod and a mediocre rod was astounding.

Gary Loomis, founder of the company, once told me, "The only expensive Loomis rod you will buy is the first one." In other words, once you realize the value of your purchase, the cost doesn't seem so much. And he's right.

If you can afford it, buy good rods, whether from Loomis or one of the other companies with a reputation for quality.

Weights

SECRET Go with tungsten. It's more expensive than lead, but it's also smaller, harder, and more sensitive to vibrations. That means that it moves more freely through cover than lead and that it magnifies the feeling of a bite. Also, it's more environmentally friendly.

SECRET Peg your bullet weight or use a screw-in version when fishing heavy grass. It will cut more easily through the cover.

SECRET Peg your sinkers with orthodontic rubber bands. Basically they are ¼-inch O-rings.

"I insert a piece of monofilament line, about 5 or 6 inches long, into the 'O' and double the line to form a needle," says Judy Wong. "Then I thread the point into the top of the sinker and pull down until the rubber band is in the middle of the sinker. Finally, I pull on one tag end and discard the line. For larger sinkers, sometimes two rubber bands are needed."

SECRET When the wind is blowing and/or the water is rough, you're better off using a weight that is too heavy than one that is too light. Otherwise, you'll never feel the bite.

SECRET Some pros insist on using painted weights that match the color of their soft plastics. They believe the consistency is more effective in attracting fish.

SECRET "Use a 1-ounce Carolina rig weight or jig to feel bottom structure in new water." —Rick Lillegard

SECRET "Add a 12-ounce teardrop lead weight to marker buoys." —Rick Lillegard

5

Tonight and Tomorrow

From dusk until dawn, the August night was ablaze and beautiful.

First, Jesse, my 13-year-old Little Brother, and I built a crackling little fire, with warmth that was welcome on this unusually cool evening. The hot dogs charred quickly. We used buns to pull them off the sticks and then slathered them with mustard. They had just the right amount of wood-smoke flavor. Ursa the Devil Dog stayed close in the firelight, in hopes of finding a fallen crumb.

An inviting sunset, fireflies, and meteor showers kept the August night ablaze and beautiful.

Then we loaded the boat with fishing tackle and paddled out into the starry, but as yet moonless night. We left a lantern on shore to light our way back and to assure Ursa that we would return. She wouldn't hear of it.

About 20 feet out, we heard a "kersplash!" I shined a flashlight beam on two glowing doggie eyes, as Ursa paddled determinedly toward us. I had taken her for rides on other days, and she inferred that we somehow must have forgotten her this time. She circled the boat, whining, until we lifted her aboard.

She did the doggie shake, giving us a Saturday night shower in lieu of a bath. Our laughter carried out over the quiet water. Now we smelled of wood smoke *and* wet dog.

Farther away from my property, darkness thickened, and I turned on a small electric lantern. Tiny yellow mayflies flocked to it—and bats followed. They swooped and dived all around us, occasionally lightly touching our lines with a wing. A typical boy, Jesse thought that was pretty neat. Ursa checked under the seats for a pith helmet.

Jesse caught the first bass, and I quickly followed with another, as we glided past the small dam.

And then we saw them. All along the wooded shoreline in front of us, fireflies blinked in the shoreline grasses, hoping to attract others of their kind for a little Saturday night frolic. Except for the dam, they circled the lake with delicate green fire, and we followed their beacons as we fished. It was wondrous.

The fishing was good, too. During the next hour or so, Jesse pulled in one bass after another on his red plastic worm—until he cast it into the sticky branches of a tree. A hard jerk broke the line.

"Just put on another," I said.

"I didn't bring any," said Jesse. "They're all back at the dock."

SECRET Never, ever, go fishing with just one of any bait, but especially soft plastics. If you do, a corollary of Murphy's Law dictates that you will lose it in a tree. I knew that, but Jesse was just a beginner. My fault for not teaching him such wisdom.

And the red worm was Jesse's "confidence" bait. He didn't want to try anything from my tackle box.

"That's okay," he said. "I think that I'm ready to go in. Are there any hot dogs left?"

With the remaining hot dogs consumed, we spread out our sleeping bags and relaxed, ready to watch the meteor showers that were predicted for after midnight.

We talked about bass fishing and building fires and other "guy things" until the first fiery arrow streaked across the sky. The wattage of the moon probably stole much of the light show from us. But we counted a dozen or so before Ursa cuddled up to Jesse. He put his head next to hers, and both slept the sleep of the innocent.

As I watched for more of nature's fireworks, I thought about another child, decades before, and how lucky he was to know generous adults who made the time to take him fishing.

My father didn't fish, but a coworker of his did, and he took me frequently to a farm pond. One fall day, a 3-pound bass exploded under my Hula Popper, a moment frozen in time that still causes my heart to pound when I recall it.

And there were others: A neighbor took me fishing in a boat for the first time. A family friend invited me along on an overnight camping and fishing trip. I've been fishing thousands of times since then, but those generous acts still are as vivid in my mind as the day they happened. I feel the sun as it warms the orange lifejacket that I wore. I look down and see the purple worm with the propeller harness tied to the line on my Johnson spincast reel. I smell the coffee brewed over a fire and see the mist at sunrise on the tailwaters of Bagnell Dam.

I hope that Jesse will have the same types of memories of our trips when he is an adult. And, when he comes of age, I hope that he will share the sport that we both love with someone new.

Bass fishing gets better when you pass it on. Take a child fishing.

SECRET You should do the same. Better bass fishing is more than about just the know-how that you accumulate. It's also about what you pass on.

Once upon a time, fathers did a good job of doing that. In a survey of anglers, 67 percent said that their fathers took them on their first fishing trips. But 87.8 percent of those respondents were age 35 or older. Of those under 35, just 12.2 percent said that they were taken by their fathers.

"If dad has a diminishing role in introducing new anglers today, and others don't step in, how will fishing be passed to future generations? And how will those who miss out even know what they've missed?" asks the Recreational Boating and Fishing Foundation, which sponsors Anglers' Legacy, an angler recruitment program.

Without participation, without a strong constituency, we will lose it all: funding for fisheries research and management; access to lakes, rivers, and oceans; an innovative industry that constantly improves our boats, tackle, and equipment.

As my eyes grew heavy, the meteors faded as the eastern sky lightened and a hidden sun painted delicate clouds a soft rose. I slept, but only for a few minutes. The angler in me would not allow for more.

I woke Jesse in time for the topwater bite.

SECRET If you night-fish on a relatively clear lake for largemouth

The Punisher hair jig is one of the best baits for smallmouth at night.

and spotted bass, try Jesse's red worm. More accurately, it's a Gene Larew red worm with gold flake, rigged Texas style. My friend Norm Klayman, arguably the best angler on Bull Shoals Lake, introduced me to it more than 20 years ago, and it still is his go-to bait for night fishing in summer. I've found it just as productive on other waters.

SECRET If you're fishing for smallmouth bass, Punisher hair jigs are hard to beat. They're made by Stephen Headrick, the "Smallmouth Guru" of Dale Hollow Lake, using the same synthetic hair that adorns life-size furry critters at Disney amusement parks. The fine hair repels water instead of absorbing it, and that allows it to flare, giving the jig more lifelike action.

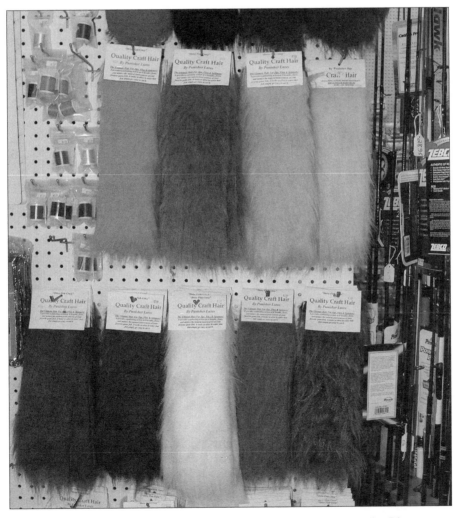

Punisher jigs are made from the same synthetic hair used to make Disney costumes.

SECRET You're more likely to catch largemouths under a full moon than smallmouths, according to Headrick.

"People like to fish during a full moon because they can see better," he says. "But that's when smallmouths get out in open water and are harder to catch."

The best night fishing for smallmouth occurs between the new and the half moon," he adds, "because smallmouths don't need as much light to feed as largemouths."

SECRET Under a bright moon in deep canyon reservoirs such as Dale Hollow Lake, baitfish often will move to shade for protection from predators. Smallmouths will follow.

SECRET Fishing at night will make you a better angler. With vision limited to the light at the boat, you're more inclined to watch your line in that light. Do that enough, and you will realize what the pros know: Sometimes you don't feel the bite, but you can see it, if you are watching closely. Too many anglers fall into the rut of depending solely on feel to detect a bass bite.

Under a bright moon, baitfish often will move into shade to hide from predators. Bass follow.

6

Strategies and Techniques

As the longtime editor of *Bassmaster* and now the senior director of publications for BASS, Dave Precht has fished with more pros, guides, and other expert anglers than I. He's an excellent angler himself, and a keen observer of what's going on around him.

When I asked him to share a secret for better bass fishing, he told me, "It's all in the retrieve."

Here is what he meant:

"Anyone who says to his fishing companion, 'We're competing against the fish, not each other,' is already several bass ahead of his buddy.

"The only times I've had such an advantage over a boatmate have been when I was getting first shot at cover (the main reason I invested in my own boat), and when I happened onto a slight nuance in the presentation my buddy hadn't yet discovered.

"Unless both fishermen figure out the precise casting angle, retrieve, cadence, or other subtle twist in presentation, action can get lopsided in a hurry.

"I was on the receiving end of such a whipping recently until my buddy, Dick Hart of Dallas, explained that he was catching scads of smallmouth by yo-yoing his lipless crankbait. We were fishing the Columbia River on the Oregon/Washington border, and a steady retrieve, at any speed, wasn't working. A stop-and-go pattern brought an occasional strike. But the only sure way to catch 'em was to stop the bait, let it fall to the top of a submerged grassbed, then lift it and drop it again. Strikes came on the fall.

"On a river in Alabama years ago, I got several fish ahead of my partner for the day by swimming small Sassy Shad grubs (the predecessor of modern swimbaits) across a sandbar. We were both using identical lures and light line and the same steady retrieve. The difference? My spinning reel was an antiquated Mitchell 308, while my friend used a more modern reel with a much faster retrieve ratio. When he slowed way down, he began to catch fish as well.

"Based on these and literally hundreds of similar experiences, I've come to believe that the way a lure is retrieved is more important sometimes than the lure itself. It's certainly more critical than color.

"Discovering the right retrieve is no different than pinpointing other elements of the presentation. It requires a little experience and a lot of trial-and-error.

"It's best, of course, if at least two people are fishing together and trying different things. When both are consciously working to refine the pattern, one is bound to hit upon the right combination sooner or later. When fishing by yourself, start out in what seems to be the most likely area, and alternately try different retrieves with the lures best suited for the conditions.

"Over the years, I've learned that certain subtle tricks work fairly consistently, and I start off with these.

"Let's start with the cast. More often than not, I get more bites when my lure lands softly. This requires a low-trajectory cast, such as pitching or flipping when presenting a jig or soft plastic lure to a precise target. For spinnerbaits and crankbaits aimed at cover, an underhand roll cast lets the lure settle almost silently into the water.

"The next key is to let the lure drop on semi-taut line for a couple of seconds. I let bottom-bouncing lures go to the bottom, of course, but subsurface lures like spinnerbaits, lipless crankbaits, and soft jerkbaits seem to catch more fish when I pause briefly before beginning my retrieve. I theorize that the splashdown mimics a surface strike. Any fish in the area senses the commotion, and then notices the lure drifting toward the bottom as if it were stunned. When the lure suddenly starts moving again, the bass moves in for the kill.

"Experience has also taught me that bass rarely prefer a consistent, steady motion over an erratic one. With a spinnerbait, I frequently jerk the bait forward during the retrieve, then pause while I take up line. During the pause, the bait stops, its skirt billows out, and the tandem blades click together. Bass can't resist it.

"I treat crankbaits the same way. Choosing a bait that runs deep enough to dig along the bottom, I crank it to maximum depth, and then I pull it with the rod tip, alternately stopping while I take up slack. Bass like the stop-and-go pattern, plus I feel more bites while moving the bait with the rod than with the reel handle.

"There's a myriad of other subtle things you can do to bass lures to make them appear more lifelike, and you should try one after another until bass respond. At that point, it's a matter of being alert enough to recognize what triggered the strike, and repeating that action. Professional anglers do this naturally—I have to force myself to focus on the retrieve.

"Admittedly, the retrieve is only one part of the presentation puzzle. But to me, it's the most important one."

SECRET Never discount beginner's luck when trying to figure out the correct retrieve.

Years ago, when I was a high school teacher, I took one of my students winter fishing with me to Bull Shoals Lake. There we joined my friend Norm Klayman, winner of many tournaments on that White River impoundment. Both Norm and I knew to bounce our grubs slowly along the bottom, as we fished the warmer water near a spring. That was a technique that had worked repeatedly for us in the past.

We explained the retrieve to Randy, my student, and then went fishing. As Norm and I struck out, Randy caught fish after fish, including a 6-pounder.

Exasperated, I decided to watch instead of fish. I quickly learned that Randy wasn't bouncing his grub, as we had instructed. Instead, he was dragging it on the bottom. Norm and I started dragging, and we caught fish.

SECRET Striking is the way that fish talk to anglers, says Emily Shaffer.

"Once that has happened, I can refine my bait. I have been with people who use a lure for 10 casts and then cut it off and change. I try to give the fish a chance to tell me what and how they want a bait.

"If I'm reeling in a jig or worm and a fish hits it on the way in, that tells me they want something moving, and I will change to a spinnerbait or a crankbait," Shaffer explains. "If I'm throwing a moving bait and I catch a fish right at the boat, that tells me to move out and fish deeper. Fish talk to us all the time. It's important to pick up on the language."

SECRET The pros share information regarding retrieves, baits, and other specifics. Sure, they're a bit secretive during a high-dollar tournament. But, in general, they are much more helpful to each other than are anglers in local bass clubs.

Yes, a few of them might have "secret" baits that they won't reveal, but stories about such lures usually are more fiction than reality.

Exchange knowledge with your buddies about where, when, and

how the bass are biting. Share effective baits when you have extras. You'll all be better off for it.

SECRET Look for the missing ingredients.

"I appreciate the pros as much as or more than anyone, but when they share tips on really whacking 'em, I am always looking for what they left out," says tournament angler Bill Frazier.

Those omissions could be intentional, but more likely they are not. When you know a process intimately, you are more likely to leave out elements that you believe to be common knowledge, but probably are not.

SECRET To ensure your continued good health, never carry just one of any bait. If you do, Murphy's Law of Angling dictates that bait will be the only one that the fish want. The revelation that you do not have another to share will not sit well with your partner who watches you boat bass after bass.

Bait Size

SECRET "A good rule of thumb for jigs and plastics is to go with bulkier baits from winter into early spring, and smaller baits in summer into early fall. It's more energy efficient for a bass to consume a bigger bait in a single attack when the water is colder. When the water is warmer, a bass will take smaller baits because it doesn't have as much need to build up reserves of energy." —Troy Gibson

SECRET Matching your lure to the size of the forage that bass are feeding on is a key to success almost anytime, but especially in the fall.

SECRET The size bait that you decide to use will depend upon many variables—time of year, depth of water, what the bass are feeding on, even what you have available in your tackle box—but here are some general guidelines from the fisheries researchers at Berkley:

Use big baits in murky water, in warm water, in thick cover, at night, when bass are active, and when you're after big bass.

Use small baits in clear water, in cold water, in sparse cover, in bright light, where bass are small, and when bass are inactive following cold fronts or when fishing pressure is heavy.

SECRET For night fishing, think big. "Its mass seems to attract fish," says pro Jay Yelas, who likes to throw a 10-inch worm.

"Moreover, the biggest bass feed primarily at night during summer, and they're ready for a big bait. In some clear lakes and reservoirs, big worms work extremely well, fished outside the deep weed line."

Buzzbaits

Have you heard of the "duck" bite? Neither had I until my friend Bill Frazier told me about it. Bill is a tournament-angling geek from North Carolina who catches more than his share of fish. For this particular pattern, he prefers Bill Norman buzzbaits with metal blades.

I'll let him tell you the rest. Hang on. It's a wild ride.

"The duck bite happens when large female bass have spawned and should be heading out for deep water. Instead, some of them go hunting baby geese or ducks.

"The baby Canada geese are just hatching out, and the shad spawn is on. You want to look for rocks and open grassland, like a pasture or golf course. The bass naturally come up after the shad, but, if you are sharp, you'll key on the nesting geese along the same rocks.

"I do not know how the bass figure out where the nests are and know those babies are about to make their first swim. You hear people talk about turtles getting the babies, but they are wrong. I've caught five bass weighing close to 40 pounds on this pattern, and a 30-pound bag is fairly easy when you hit it right. Four of those fish in the 40-pound sack came from a spot about the size of a bushel basket, 5 feet in front of a goose nest.

"I try to match the hatch with my buzzbait. If I'm fishing near a momma duck and her babies, I'll switch to a smaller bait and add more brown, pumpkin, or black to the skirt.

"If I'm fishing something like primrose or wide beds of water willow, I'll go to a triple blade. That helps keep it from rolling over and catching the weed.

"I always use metal blades. With rivets and beads, I'll make modifications to make the buzzbait scream like a banshee. I want it to sound like a baby that has gotten separated from momma and is scatting along to find her. I know you've seen them do this.

"Tuning and cadence are keys, and everything has to be just right to score huge. I've only put it together just right maybe two or three times in the 10 years since I discovered it.

"The absolute truth of the matter is that all the details of lures and presentation came from articles and television shows, most of them *Bassmaster*. All I did was connect the dots with the goose/duck component, and that was sheer dumb luck of being in the right place at the right time for the fish to show it to me."

SECRET When fishing the shad spawn on riprap, make your buzzbait tick the rocks for added attraction.

SECRET "Buzzbait anglers can increase the noise and productivity of their lures by replacing the metal rivet on the back of the bait with one a size larger. Hardware stores carry a wide selection of rivets. Also, before placing the new rivet on the lure, soak it in salt water overnight and then allow it to dry. The corrosion on the rivet will significantly increase the noise of the bait." —Matt Beck

SECRET To cast a small, light buzzbait farther, clamp a rubber-core sinker onto the hook shaft.

SECRET Buzzbaits aren't just for hot weather. You also should try them during spring and fall, especially on unseasonably warm days, when bass might move into shallow water to feed.

SECRET Don't make the mistake of just "covering water" with a buzzbait. As with many other baits, cast to specific places, where fish might be holding.

SECRET "Large, loud, and fast" aren't always the best for buzzbait fishing. Sometimes, bass want a smaller, slower, and/or more subtle bait.

Color

SECRET In deciding what color lure to use, look at the water. If it's clear, you probably want to use light colors such as white, chrome, or pearl. Use yellow or chartreuse in stained water, and the brightest or darkest colors—orange, brown, black—in muddy water.

SECRET "During the prespawn and spawn, throw a lure with some red on it." —Brooks Rogers

Actually, red might be beneficial just about anytime. Many anglers believe that a little red around the head of the bait or on the belly triggers aggressive behavior from bass. Biologists say that may be because the fish associate red with injured prey, fights for dominance, and spawning.

If you want to find out for yourself, use a waterproof marker or fingernail polish to put a little red around the gills, along the belly, or even on the tail of your favorite crankbait. Or try using a spinnerbait with red blades instead of the traditional silver or gold.

SECRET Sometimes, color means very little. Lure designer Sam Griffin field tests his wooden topwater baits without painting them. He catches plenty of bass with them, too. He says that color matters more to anglers than it does to fish.

SECRET Instead of using colors that they've heard are hot on a particular lake, many pros rely instead on what has worked in the past under similar circumstances and in similar waters.

SECRET Sometimes the right color is a color that the fish haven't seen before, and thus haven't become accustomed to. How else do you explain the success of anglers who use bubblegum-pink floating worms?

SECRET Just how well fish see colors still is a mystery. But fisheries experts believe that their ability to detect color differences and contrasts falls short of our own. That's good news for those anglers who worry about fish seeing their line, and not so good news for those who believe that catching bass can be as easy as choosing the right color for a worm, crankbait, or spinnerbait.

SECRET If bass are following your crankbait or jerkbait, but not striking, maybe the color is too "hot" or bright. Switch to something more subdued.

SECRET If you are fishing for bedding bass, it's more important to throw a color that *you* can see. That way you know where your bait is in relation to the fish, and you can see the take. The same holds true when bass want a floating worm, which explains why bubblegum-pink, white, and bright yellow are popular options.

Crankbaits

SECRET No matter where you are going fishing or what you are going to fish for, take along some Rat-L-Traps or Super Spots. These lipless crankbaits will catch just about everything that swims, from bass to tarpon. Best colors include gold with black back and chrome with blue back.

SECRET Most large peacock bass are caught on topwater baits. But if you are going fishing for them, take lipless crankbaits also. You'll want to take a break occasionally from throwing and retrieving a big bait. Also, lipless crankbaits will catch peacock bass, as well as a greater variety of other fish, including piranhas.

SECRET "When fishing crankbaits, pay attention to what size line you are using. For instance, a No. 6 Fat Free Shad will run about a foot deeper on 10-pound line than it will on 12-pound-test." —Tim Horton, pro angler

SECRET Don't hesitate to throw a crankbait in a "baby bass" pattern. Bass do eat their young.

SECRET Sticking your rod tip in the water while retrieving a crankbait will make your bait run deeper, as well as reduce the bow in your line.

SECRET To "tune" a crankbait, use pliers to slightly bend the line-tie

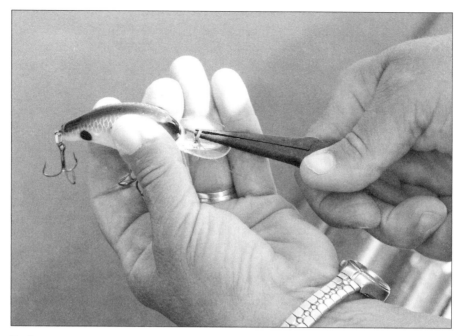

To "tune" a crankbait, slightly bend the line-tie eye in the opposite direction from the way the bait has been running.

eye of the lure in the opposite direction from the way the bait has been running. For example, if the lure tracks too much to the left, twist the eye to the right.

SECRET Sometimes, you might want to bend the bill so that a crankbait *does run* to the left or right. That can be beneficial for running under the ledges on a cliff wall or the edges of a dock.

SECRET You can make a lipless crankbait more weedless and add vibration by removing the rear treble hook.

SECRET To make a lipless crankbait run silent, drill a hole in the nose of the lure in front of the hook hanger and squeeze some glue into the hole. That should freeze the front steel ball in place.

SECRET Check the hooks before you throw a new crankbait. Some are dull and/or too small. That's why many of the pros take off the standard hooks that come on some crankbaits and put on larger and sharper versions. A few companies equip their baits with premium hooks.

SECRET Not all crankbaits are equal. Even though a crankbait is the identical brand and model of the one that you've used to catch hundreds of bass, it might not run the same. That's why an old, battered bait with all the paint worn off sometimes catches more bass than a glittery, new version.

Fighting the Fish

SECRET Don't use the same hookset for a crankbait that you would for a plastic worm. Instead of cranking the line tight and then slamming home the hook with the rod as you would when fishing soft plastic, set the hook by reeling against the resistance of the fish. This helps you catch up with the bass and also applies enough pressure so that the fish will resist, and, in so doing, drive the hooks in even deeper.

SECRET "Fishing heavy cover for largemouth bass can create a multitude of problems for anglers. In the excitement of battling a giant fish in the weeds or wood, many times the natural tendency is to keep pulling until the bass is free from the cover. Most often, this simply pulls the hook from the fish's mouth. It also can straighten a hook, even an extra-strong hook. Instead, after a strong hookset is used to gain control of the fish's head, simply wedge the fish against the cover and use the trolling motor to go after the fish, applying only enough pressure to keep a good, tight line. Odds are, fewer fish will be lost." —Matt Beck

SECRET To keep a hooked fish from jumping, push your rod tip into the water and keep a tight line.

SECRET As you work a big fish closer to the boat, carefully back off on the drag. That way, if it makes a hard, frantic run, it is not as likely to break the line.

SECRET In fact, train yourself to back off on your drag immediately after you hook a bass and move it into open water. Then use your thumb as a drag as you bring the fish to the boat.

SECRET Once a fish is near the boat, the extreme angle from reel to fish creates a resistance that basically negates the drag. That's when the cushioning action of the rod takes over and you use that to tire out the fish. But always be ready to lower the rod tip and allow your thumb or loose drag to release line when that bass of a lifetime decides to make one final lunge.

SECRET Set your drag looser with braided lines than you would with monofilament. If the drag is set too tight, braided line will tend to bury itself in the coils on the spool when you set the hook, especially if a big fish is on the other end. When that happens close enough to the boat, a 10- or maybe even a 5-pound bass can pop 80-pound braided line.

SECRET Never use the net to try to grab the bass. Instead, push the net down into the water and lead the fish headfirst into it.

SECRET Despite what you see the pros do, swinging a bass into the boat is not a good idea. A fish that flops around on the deck and loses

When fighting a fish in heavy cover, don't pull too hard to bring it through the grass.

its protective slime coating is far more likely to develop a fatal bacterial infection later on.

Also, you just might break your rod if that fish is too large or decides to jerk at just the right moment. I've seen this happen several times.

Instead, lip the fish, cradle it under the belly, or net it, preferably with a rubber net that has no knots in it.

SECRET You also risk breaking the rod if you jerk it past 90 degrees with resistance (fish or hangup) on the other end of the line.

Jerkbaits

SECRET Because jerkbaits attract fish visually, you'll do better with them on sunny days. The sun gives the bait flash and also creates a silhouette that the fish can see from below.

SECRET Early and late and on cloudy days, a gold shade often works best. Go with natural/silver with sun hitting the water.

SECRET "One of the best lures for winter and early spring bass is the Countdown Rapala. Work the lure slowly and vary the retrieve for optimum appeal. Smaller minnow baits in darker finishes seem to be the most effective for coldwater situations." —Sid Montgomery

SECRET During winter, you can't fish a suspending jerkbait too slowly. If you aren't getting bites, chances are good that you're not giving lethargic bass time to move up to the bait.

Jigs and Spoons

SECRET "Use Super Glue to stiffen the weed guard on a jig that you're fishing in heavy cover." —Rick Lillegard

SECRET "Trim the weed guard on a jig for use in sparse cover." —Rick Lillegard

SECRET "To help a jig penetrate heavy weeds, shave the pork trailer thinner with a razor blade." —Rick Lillegard

SECRET "Add a Hula Grub to a living rubber jig. The double skirt allows bulk for skipping, and also allows the jig to fall slowly." —Rick Lillegard

SECRET "When fishing a worm or jig in cool water, throw as light a lure as you can." —Brooks Rogers

SECRET "To get a fish's attention, knock a jig into dock posts or trees." —Rick Lillegard

SECRET "For heart-pounding strikes, scurry a ¼-ounce jig with a larger trailer over heavy weeds or pads. Allow it to fall into any holes. Use a heavy rod and line and hold on!" —Rick Lillegard

SECRET Modify that pork trailer to give your jig-and-pig a different look and action, which could be just what the bass are waiting for. Use a punch to put holes in the legs or split each of them up to the fat part of the body.

SECRET Sometimes, a horizontal retrieve of a spoon is more effective than a vertical one. This is especially true if the fish are moving

For heart-pounding strikes, scurry a light jig with a trailer over heavy weeds and pads.

or suspended. Cast the spoon, allow it to touch bottom, and then pop it sharply. If you don't draw a strike, reel in a little line and pop the bait again. Keep up the technique all the way to the boat.

Presentation

SECRET Be patient. Your first cast to a likely looking spot almost always provides your best opportunity to catch a bass at that place. More often than not, the fish is just sitting there, looking for a meal to swim by. That's why you should wait until you are in perfect position to make the perfect cast. If you cast all around the area as you approach, you might catch the bass or, just as likely, you might frighten it and make it more difficult—or even impossible—to catch.

SECRET Cast past the cover that you think might be holding fish. That way, you won't frighten the fish, and, when your bait nears the target area, it will be at the proper depth or "strike zone."

SECRET "After several presentations across a point from various angles, find the slack-water area of the point—the backside of the point out of the direct moving water. Some of the area's biggest fish could be holding here, waiting for food to wash by." —Matt Beck

SECRET "Fish vertically in heavy current." —Rick Lillegard

SECRET "Windblown banks are good places to catch bass. That's because the waves stir up microorganisms and wash them out for minnows, shad, and crayfish to eat. These forage species then draw in bass

Bass sometimes will concentrate on windblown banks.

Birds often will help you find bass that are schooling and feeding.

and other predators, which look toward the bank to feed. If you don't get bites by fishing a windblown bank from one angle, then approach it from another and another until you find the fish." —Troy Gibson

SECRET "If you see schooling fish, they are feeding, and you probably can catch them by throwing baits into their midst. But if you're making casts to stumps or brushpiles and not getting bitten, then you might need to aggravate the fish into striking. I like to do that by making multiple casts to the same spot with a crankbait or spinnerbait and retrieving aggressively." —Troy Gibson

SECRET Under an overcast sky, you're more likely to catch bass on fast-moving crankbaits or spinnerbaits. Under a bright sky, the fish will hold tighter to cover, and you generally will have better luck with jigs and soft plastics.

SECRET Remember to bounce your crankbait or spinnerbait off a stump or log as your retrieve it. That erratic action can trigger a strike.

SECRET Most strikes occur within the first third of your retrieve. That means it usually makes sense to get a worm or jig quickly back to the boat, after you've retrieved it out of the strike zone. This will allow you to make more casts, thus increasing your odds of catching fish.

SECRET If you see a bass following your bait, stop it immediately. With any luck, that will trigger a strike. The technique works especially well with a suspending jerkbait. Let it sit for a few seconds if the bass doesn't hit. Then twitch it. That slight movement also can prompt a bite.

SECRET Possibly the largest strike zone for bass occurs in the pre-spawn period in spring. This is when the fish are shallow and will chase fast-moving lures such as crankbaits and spinnerbaits.

SECRET Pay close attention to that first strike of the day. It can tell you how aggressive the fish are and how they are positioned in relation to cover.

SECRET If you catch bass with a worm, try a spinnerbait or crankbait in the same spot and at the same depth. If the fish don't want a fast-moving bait, you always can go back to the worm.

SECRET "The speed of your retrieve and the depth of the lure often are more important than the color of the bait." —Brooks Rogers

SECRET To become a better angler, forget about distance when casting and concentrate on accuracy.

SECRET "Many bass anglers who employ the shallow-water technique of flipping have found that running their trolling motors at a constant low speed while fishing, instead of turning the motor on and off, improves their catch rates." —Matt Beck

SECRET For flipping and pitching, you should combine accurate casts with an ability to quickly determine which exact spot is the best place to drop or pitch a bait as your boat moves along the shoreline. The faster you can make these decisions, the more effective your presentations will be and the more bass that you will catch.

Successful flipping and pitching requires accuracy and an ability to quickly read the water.

Skipping baits under docks is a good way to catch bass on heavily pressured lakes.

SECRET Set up an elevated platform at home to practice pitching. That way the motion will become more instinctive and you can concentrate on finding the best targets when you go fishing.

SECRET An underhand cast allows for a much quieter presentation of your lure and increases your chances of catching fish that are holding tight to cover in shallow water.

SECRET "For improved accuracy and less intrusive bait delivery, learn to feather the line with your index finger when fishing with spinning reels." —Rick Lillegard

SECRET Skipping baits under docks is one of the best ways to catch bass on lakes that are heavily pressured and have lots of boat traffic.

You can "skip" with a baitcaster or a spinning outfit. Either way, the key is practice, practice, practice, until you can put a lure 20 feet under a dock. Also, remember to use a smooth, fluid motion. Do *not* start, stop, and then try to shoot the bait forward.

SECRET If you're going to skip a bait, peg the weight or use an internal weight or jighead.

SECRET "Round-edge baits such as tubes and baits without legs and tails are much easier to skip under docks. Those with sharp edges and/or appendages dig into or stick onto the surface of the water, slowing them down and limiting their effectiveness." —Rick Lillegard

Rivers and Streams

SECRET Bend down the barbs on the hooks of those small crankbaits that you use in streams to catch panfish, smallmouth bass, and trout. You'll still catch them, but the tiny hooks will be much easier to remove from the fish—and your own flesh.

SECRET Walking or wading upstream often is the best way to fish. This allows you to give your fly or lure a more natural presentation, as it moves with the current.

SECRET "River anglers and those accustomed to fishing moving water know the importance of bringing a lure to the boat in line with the current's direction. Bass and other gamefish are opportunistic feeders that position themselves facing into the current, waiting for an easy meal to be washed in their direction." —Matt Beck

Wading against the current is the best way to fish a stream.

SECRET "Bass relate to the seasons very predictably, behaving the same year after year when circumstances such as weather conditions and water levels are similar." —Lee Bailey

SECRET "River bass usually are less susceptible to cold fronts than are their counterparts in lakes." —Lee Bailey

River anglers know the importance of retrieving their baits in line with the current's direction.

Seasonal

SECRET During winter, bass typically relate more to bait than cover. They're likely to be holding in deep water along steep banks and channel bends.

SECRET "Rivers and river-system lakes offer some of the best early season bass fishing, especially if you are pursuing smallmouth bass. River systems will have open water, while many lakes in northern regions will just be thawing. As water temperatures and river levels rise, bass and their forage begin an early season feed.

"Temperatures reaching the mid to upper 50s usually will trigger major bass activity through a river system. Occasionally, river smallmouths will begin their spawning rituals before the temperatures reach the low 50s. As a rule of thumb, anglers should pay particular attention to water temperatures that rise four or five degrees, especially if the rise occurs over a period of only a few days." —Lee Bailey

Soft Plastics

SECRET "Careful consideration should be made when choosing the proper hook for a soft plastic lure. Remember that the larger the diameter of the hook, the more force is needed to penetrate the mouth of a fish. Small, light-wire hooks are best for light line, such as 4- to 10-pound test, while 3/0 and larger hooks work best with lines in the heavier 14- to 25-pound class. Anglers using the new generation of braided superlines should consider using stout XXX-strong hooks in size 3/0 and up. Lighter hooks can bend or break under stress from braided line." —Matt Beck

The use of light-wire hooks, of course, necessitates the use of smaller and often thinner plastics. Line, hook, and bait all should complement one another.

SECRET "For newcomers to bass fishing or children who have less hook-setting power, use a 1/0 hook instead of the larger, thicker hooks. Why? Which is easier to pierce through a piece of leather? A needle or a nail? The 1/0 hook is like a needle and sets much easier with less pressure. But you must adjust the reel drag tight enough without being so tight that the hook will bend on the hookset. With the drag properly adjusted, the hook will penetrate instead of bend." —Kathy Magers

SECRET "When using soft plastics, always make sure that the gap of your hook is wide enough to allow for free and unimpeded hooksets. Many anglers use hooks with too narrow gaps." —Dave Burkhardt

SECRET Push a hook barb out the top of the worm about halfway down, twist it, and simply "skin" the barb beneath the outer layer of the lure's belly to keep it weedless, says Kathy Magers.

"This allows for a very easy hookset that requires much less power than when the barb is buried deep within the core of the lure."

SECRET "Use spray on lures not only for an attractant but also to help the lure slide through cover." —Rick Lillegard

SECRET "Use Super Glue to fasten soft plastic trailers to the hook shank." —Rick Lillegard

SECRET "Some of the best soft plastic jerkbaits on the market are made very soft. Sometimes one bite from a fish is all that's needed to tear the bait, rendering it useless. A tube of Super Glue can give you more life from these baits. Place a drop or two of glue where the hook comes out the head of the bait, which is the area that tears most often. This will allow the lure to be fished again and again." —Matt Beck

SECRET When using a soft jerkbait in open water, catch those bass that are striking short by sliding a No. 2 treble onto the shank of the main hook before you push the barb through the bait.

SECRET After you put the hook through the head of a soft jerkbait, put two small nuts onto the shank of your wide-gap hook, before sticking the barb into the body of the bait. The added weight will give the bait a slow fall and a more natural look. Also, the nuts will click together, giving your bait fish-attracting noise.

SECRET Insert a rattle into your soft plastic bait if the bite is slow. Sometimes a little noise is all that's needed to get a fish's attention.

SECRET Use plastic beads with tungsten bullet weights. Tungsten is so hard that it will shatter glass beads.

SECRET Go through soft plastics annually and throw out old ones. Oil separates from baits over time, and old baits turn hard and impede hooksets.

SECRET "Instead of throwing away lizards, Hula Grubs, and small soft plastics like Zoom Critter Craws, pinch off the damaged head and save the remainder of these lures for trailers on small jigs. The compact look often draws strikes from leery post-frontal bass." —Kathy Magers

SECRET The "plastic lizard," a favorite among many bass anglers, really imitates a salamander—the adult and larval stages of the tiger salamander—instead of a lizard. It's doubtful that bass attack plastic lizards so ferociously because the real amphibians eat fish eggs and fish have an instinctive hatred for them. In truth, salamanders prey on insects. And bass, in turn, simply like to eat "lizards," particularly in spring, when they are more abundant.

"Lizards" aren't really lizards, but bass still like to eat them.

SECRET The drop-shot rig is the closest an angler can get to fishing live bait for bass, without actually using live bait. Many pros consider it the best way to catch deepwater bass.

Rigs vary from angler to angler, but here are the basics: Tie a weight (usually from ⅛ ounce to ¼ ounce) to the end of your line. Then, using a Palomar knot, tie a 1/0 or smaller hook above the weight. When properly attached, the hook should be perpendicular to the line. Distance between sinker and hook can be anywhere from 6 inches to 4 or 5 feet, depending on how bass are relating to bottom structure and baitfish.

Finally, hook a finesse worm through the nose, or wacky-style (through the middle of the body with the hook point exposed).

The best way to work this rig is to allow the worm to fall weightlessly on a slack line, after the sinker has touched bottom. Some anglers like to shake the rod to make the bait dance, but a raise-and-drop probably is more effective for bass that aren't aggressively feeding. Another option is to hold the line taut and allow underwater currents to flutter the bait.

SECRET When fishing is tough, try fishing a worm wacky style, especially if you are working water that's 10-feet deep or less.

SECRET A 24-inch leader is adequate for most Carolina rigging. Use a little less line if the bait is small and/or the fish are especially active.

SECRET Don't yank hard when you hang up a bait using a Carolina rig. Instead, move the boat over the snag, tighten your line, and then release the spool, allowing the sinker to drop straight down and knock the lure free.

SECRET A Carolina rig often is better than a Texas rig for fishing soft plastics during windy weather. The heavier weight casts easier, gets down faster, and allows you to better keep in touch with the bottom. It also permits you to crawl the bait, in hopes of attracting sluggish fish.

SECRET "For a fast Carolina rig retie: When you break off at the swivel, slide the weight and bead up your line to the length of leader that you want. Cut the line just below them and turn the new leader around. Tie the swivel to the main line and the hook to the free end." —Lance Vick

SECRET "In general, don't use heavy line and weights, bulky beads, and oversize hooks on Carolina rigs," says pro Jan Heavener. "So many times I've seen people casting a large, oversized mass of bait that will scare off more fish than it attracts."

SECRET "If the fish are picking at your tube bait and you're having trouble hooking them, take off every other tentacle to reduce size and bulkiness. This allows the remaining tentacles to moving more freely and the tube to displace less water, for a more stealthy and natural presentation. This technique can be especially effective in clear water." —Troy Gibson

SECRET "Trim the long tentacles on tubes when sight fishing. This allows for a more subtle presentation." —Rick Lillegard

SECRET "Add action to a tube by leaving the weight free on the line so that you can pop it off the bottom." —Rick Lillegard

SECRET Tube baits catch more smallmouth bass than any other lure. Partially that's because they are effective year-round. But also they work because the subtle action of their tails seems to arouse the curiosity and pugnacious attitude of these hard fighters. Depending on the retrieve and color, a tube can resemble a baitfish or a crayfish, which is one of the smallmouth's favorite foods.

SECRET Day in and day out, pumpkin probably is the best tube color for smallmouth bass, according to Bruce Holt, executive director of the G.Loomis fishing rod company. Holt regularly fishes the Columbia River for bronzebacks. He also likes chartreuse on the tips of the tentacles. "Drag or swim the tube," he says. "Don't hop it."

Depending on color and retrieve, a tube can resemble a baitfish or a crayfish.

SECRET "When fishing soft plastics, some anglers "go on point" and wait to feel the fish hit a second time before setting the hook. Many times the fish already has the lure in its mouth and is swimming toward the boat. That means you're waiting for nothing. Take out the slack in your line and feel for the fish. Then set the hook as soon as possible. Otherwise, a bass is more likely to be 'gut-hooked.' Set the hook soon—for the fish's sake." —Kathy Magers

Spinnerbaits

SECRET "When fishing clear water, pull a few strands off the skirt of your spinnerbait and trim others in uneven lengths. This will give your bait a smaller, more natural appearance in the clear water." —Lance Vick

SECRET "When you have the need for a heavier spinnerbait without increasing the profile of the lure, try crimping a rubber-sleeved, elongated sinker behind the head of the bait for added weight. Commonly, anglers use weights in the ¼- to ½-ounce size. The additional weight will not only allow the angler to fish the bait deeper, but it will not adversely affect the action of the lure." —Matt Beck

SECRET Contrary to popular belief, a spinnerbait bite can be soft and subtle, especially on a slow retrieve. Many anglers like to fish spinnerbaits because bass often hit these baits with ferocity. Sometimes, though, a bass will swim up behind a spinnerbait and take it into its mouth with such delicacy that anglers never know that they had a bite—if they are not paying attention to slight changes in resistance or movements of the line. Devote just as much attention trying to detect bites with spinnerbaits as you do with soft plastics, and you'll catch more bass.

SECRET A spinnerbait is one of your best choices for a "search" bait. You can cover a lot of water by cranking it fast, but also slow it down around cover. Lipless crankbaits, buzzbaits, and even topwaters also are good lures to throw when you are looking for bass around visible cover.

SECRET "Chartreuse spinnerbaits with Indiana blades are good choices for smallmouth bass. For off-colored water, go with Colorado blades." —Bruce Holt

Topwaters

My name is Robert Montgomery, and I am a topwater addict. I'll fish an hour or more for just one blowup on my favorite topwater bait, the Offset Sam. Catching a big bass on it is great, of course. But, heck, I

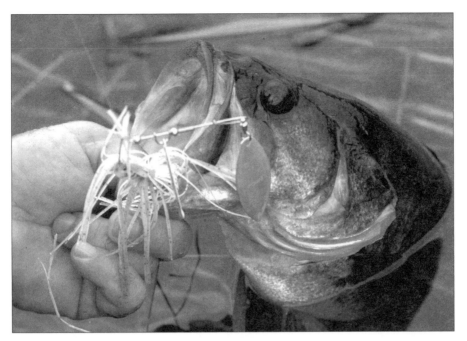

Bass don't always hit spinnerbaits with ferocity.

A spinnerbait is one of your best choices for a "search" bait.

don't even have to do that. Just seeing and hearing that explosion sends an adrenaline surge through my veins that will keep me high for hours.

And the visuals from those explosions stay with me, too. I still remember one warm, sunny afternoon on Lake El Salto in Mexico, with the water flat as glass. The bite was slow so I decided I'd throw the Offset, just for a change of pace. Neither the guide nor my partner said anything when I tied on the large propeller bait. But I could see the disbelief in their eyes. They thought that I'd been in the sun too long.

But on my third or fourth cast near a flooded fence post, a violent explosion shattered the flat water and ripped through the quiet, lazy day. The fish missed the bait, but waves from the assault rocked our boat. No one said a word. Sweat running down our faces, we just stood there and watched as the ripples slowly died away.

The maker of the Offset Sam, Sam Griffin, is of the same mindset as I.

"Keep throwing a topwater and eventually you will get bit," says the man who has been designing and making topwater lures for nearly 30 years and who has been living on and fishing Lake Okeechobee for most of his 70-plus years.

Sam Griffin has been designing and making topwater lures for nearly 30 years.

"My big things are to be confident and have patience. I'll fish behind people throwing worms and crankbaits and catch fish they bypass. I like to fish that topwater slower and let 'em read the menu."

In my opinion, no one knows more about topwater fishing than Sam, and that's why I asked him to share some of his secrets with me and you:

SECRET On topwaters, most fish are caught on the front hook. That means it is important to have a bigger, stronger hook there.

SECRET Dress up the back hook. Sam has learned that he gets 25 percent more bites when he puts pearlescent Mylar tinsel on the back hook. It's especially productive when the bait is sitting still.

SECRET The same topwater bait will work anywhere. "It's a matter of confidence," says Sam. "That's why there are regional favorites."

SECRET Slow down. "Most of the time, people fish a topwater too fast," the lure designer says. "They're just pulling and pulling. I'd say that 85 percent of the time, the bite comes when the bait is still or coming to a stop."

With most topwaters, Sam will jerk the bait twice, creating slack in the line and allowing the bait to sit. Then he will swing the rod tip toward the bait, taking in line, and repeat the sequence. With a popper, he might jerk just once.

"Pay attention and fish will let you know what they want," he says. "If you are fishing too fast, they will follow but not hit."

SECRET "Early and late is a myth," says Sam. "Those are not the only times to throw a topwater. People used to fish two or three hours before work and then come home and fish two or three hours. That's the way that got started. I've found that 10 to 2 is the most productive time for big fish."

SECRET Color is more important to the angler than it is the fish.

"When I develop a lure, I seal it so it won't take on water, but I don't paint it," Sam explains. "Then I fish with it. I've probably caught more fish on those baits than with painted baits. I've sold a few like that too, but mostly they're too bland for fishermen."

"I offer 26 colors, but black and white is what I use the most. It's what I grew up with and what I have confidence in."

SECRET Topwaters aren't just for warm water.

"You can catch bass consistently on top in water that is 50 degrees or above," the Florida native says. "Usually in colder water, you want to fish extremely fast or extremely slow, not in between."

The popper is a good choice for colder water, he adds, because you

Sam Griffin makes a variety of wooden topwater baits.

can keep it in one place longer and because its tail sits down in the water, making it easier for the bass to take.

SECRET Topwaters aren't just for calm water either.

"Take what the weather gives you," says Sam. "In rough weather, you can throw in the 'wind rows' in grass. And you can throw in troughs between waves. Most of the time, you'll want a faster retrieve in rough water, to take the slack out of your line."

SECRET Not every topwater bite is explosive. In general, louder and larger baits will draw more aggressive bites. Smaller, more subtle baits will get the "suckers."

"In cold weather and in calm water, when you're using a small bait, it's really important to watch your line, just like you would with other baits," Sam says. "That's because you're more likely to get a sucking bite.

"With a soft, suck bite on the back of the bait, don't set the hook hard," he cautions. "Instead, lift up and reel. Otherwise you'll pull the hook out. When you do get a fish this way, it's usually hooked on the edge of the mouth or even the outside."

Here are additional tips from Zell Rowland, and other topwater experts:

`SECRET` Set the hook more by what you feel than by what you see, especially when fishing buzzbaits and plastic frogs. A bass sometimes will strike at a bait two or three times before it actually gets it in its mouth.

`SECRET` And speaking of frogs . . . Because they're weedless, they're a great choice for fishing grass and weeds. But also try them in open water, where most anglers won't throw them.

`SECRET` "When you approach a target, cast your topwater first to the shady side. But always work the whole area thoroughly." —Zell Rowland

`SECRET` "When fishing clear water with a topwater bait, long casts are less likely to frighten the fish." —Zell Rowland

`SECRET` "Pay attention to the water all around your topwater bait. A bass may give away its presence by making subtle waves around your lure." —Zell Rowland

`SECRET` "Larger lures generally will stimulate larger strikes, while smaller lures will prompt more strikes." —Zell Rowland

`SECRET` "Make sure to pay attention to how you are working a topwater bait so that you can repeat the action that finally draws a strike." —Zell Rowland

`SECRET` "Bending the blades on a prop bait backward will allow it to be jerked farther and more easily through the water. Bending the blades forward creates more resistance and restricts a bait's movement." —Zell Rowland

`SECRET` Where you position the knot on the line tie of a popper will determine the type of splash that it makes. Putting it at the bottom makes the bait surge upward, creating a bigger splash. With the knot at the top, the popper is more likely to dive and gurgle.

`SECRET` "Sharp hooks are especially important on a topwater bait, since a hooked fish often will thrash around on top before making a run." —Zell Rowland

`SECRET` "Use a limber rod with topwater baits. It allows you to work the bait with more ease and allows the bass a little more time to pull the lure into its mouth when it strikes." —Zell Rowland

`SECRET` "One drawback to fishing large topwater lures such as a Heddon Zara Spook is that a hooked fish often will throw the lure after jumping. One way to combat the problem is to remove the hooks and place a medium-size split ring on them. This will take away much of the leverage a fish can use to throw the lure. A similar size split ring on the nose of the lure also will improve its action." —Matt Beck

`SECRET` Attach a popping bug to a topwater bait with 18 to 24 inches of monofilament or fluorocarbon line. This rig will catch big pan-fish as well as bass. It also will allow you to catch two fish on one cast, especially if they are feeding aggressively on top.

This was one of the first "tricks" I learned as a child, when I graduated from live bait to artificials. When I was a teen, the popping bug produced my first 5-pound-plus bass.

SECRET On a cloudy or rainy day, go with a dark topwater bait. On a sunny day, try shad or clear colors.

SECRET Bass will bite topwaters all day, even on sunny days, and especially in shallow lakes with aquatic vegetation.

SECRET Topwaters generally don't work well for bass in dingy or stained water because the fish hold tighter to cover. Spinnerbaits, jigs, and worms usually work better in this type of water.

SECRET Often the best time to throw a propeller topwater bait is an overcast day with a slight chop on the water.

Favorite Baits

*S*everal years ago, I asked professional anglers and guides this question: If you could have only one bait for catching bass, what would it be?

Not surprisingly, the jig, plastic worm, and Rat-L-Trap were the lures most often named, with the last one as the top vote getter.

The jig, of course, will catch just about anything that swims, in fresh or salt water. Additionally, it is one of the most versatile of all baits. Anglers can swim it, crawl it, or hop it along the bottom, or flip it into thick cover. Possibly most important, they can slow down the retrieve to entice bites when fish are not aggressive.

Anglers also can vary the retrieve on a worm and move it ever so slowly. Plus, a worm seems to be a "non-memory" bait for bass. In other words, fish don't seem to learn to avoid it, as they do other lures.

The negative side to these two baits is that an angler must be able to deliver a quick, hard hookset when a bass bites. That means these are not good baits for beginning anglers.

On the other hand, the Rat-L-Trap, a lipless crankbait, sometimes is referred to as an "idiot bait." That's because almost anyone can catch fish with it simply by throwing it out and reeling it in. No hookset is required, although it is recommended.

Anglers can cover a lot of water with this bait and, if they throw it long enough, almost certainly will run it close to a bass that can not resist striking on pure instinct.

Of course, some of the pros and guides had other favorites, including various types of crankbaits, spinnerbaits, topwaters, and suspending jerkbaits.

During my more than 20 years of talking and fishing with these experts all over the U.S., as well as in Mexico and Canada, I've developed my own list of favorite lures. They're baits that I never leave home

If they could have only one bait, many anglers would choose the Rat-L-Trap.

without, no matter where I'm going fishing for bass. They are my "confidence" baits, producing fish time after time for me. Except for one, they all are readily available at Bass Pro Shops and other retail outlets.

1. Rat-L-Trap by Bill Lewis Lures

If the bass aren't biting anything else, then I will throw a 'Trap or a Spot (see next page). These baits have saved countless trips for me, especially when I need a "photo" fish for a magazine article.

These lipless crankbaits will put fish in the boat—and in front of the camera—when nothing else will. One reason for this is that they cover more water than slower-moving baits, increasing the likelihood that they will swim in front of accommodating bass. Another is that their vibration and noise attract attention.

Some mistakenly believe that the 'Trap is for catching numbers of fish, instead of quality bass. Yes, that can be true if you throw a ⅛- or ¼-ounce bait. I prefer the ¾-ounce, and I've caught enough big bass with it to convince myself that the 'Trap is a good bait for trophies as well. Aside from its larger profile, the ¾-ounce model also has more rugged split rings and hooks, both important when you're catching big and/or large numbers of bass.

Be sure to check the hook points before you throw a new 'Trap. I've found that they sometimes need sharpening.

I throw chrome with black back and chrome with blue back on sunny days in clear to slightly stained water, and I go with reds or crayfish patterns before the sun is high, on cloudy days, and/or in colored water.

2. Super Spot
by Cotton Cordell

Put the 'Trap and Spot side by side and the only difference seems to be that the 'Trap has a dorsal fin. But they also differ in vibration and noise (from the rattles), which is why I always carry both. Sometimes bass seem to prefer one and other times the other.

Back in the 1990s, parent company PRADCO made some Excalibur Spots in ⅜-ounce and ⅝-ounce sizes. With those extra-sharp Excalibur trebles, they were dynamite baits for me, especially in baby bass, shad, and red-with-orange-belly patterns. In fact, I caught a 12 pound, 4-ounce large-mouth on the red-with-orange, ⅜-ounce version at Lake Guerrero.

When PRADCO stopped making that version of the Spot, I searched tackle shops, looking in vain for leftovers. Sadly, I have only a few left, and can't seem to find any more.

Also a lipless crankbait, the Super Spot varies in noise and vibration from the 'Trap.

3. X-Rap by Rapala

The tackle industry produces an abundance of good suspending jerkbaits, but this recent introduction by Rapala is my favorite. I had the good fortune to field-test it at Lake El Salto in Mexico just before it hit the market, and I have been sold on it ever since.

I like the 4-inch version, which is comparable to most other suspending minnow baits, but I especially like the 3⅛-inch model. It's a great bait when schooling bass are keying on small forage. I'm not certain if they are more attracted by the sharp darting action of the bait itself or by the Flash Foil Teaser tail as the X-Rap stops and suspends.

But I am certain that this bait catches bass.

The X-Rap is especially good for making long casts to schooling fish, despite its light weight.

The plastic worm has caught more bass than any other artificial bait.

Additionally, Rapala has incorporated an "integrated long-casting system." That means an angler can make long casts with this bait, despite its light weight. That's especially important when in pursuit of schooling bass.

My favorite colors are Glass Ghost, Hot Steel, and Clown.

4. Power Worm by Berkley and Ribbontail by YUM

Of course, any angler's list of favorite baits must include the plastic worm, a bait that has caught more bass than any other. My list is no exception, but I couldn't name just one. I like both of these.

When Berkley first started making the Power Worm, colors often were washed out and/or inconsistent. If you bought the bait, it was solely for the scent.

That's no longer the case. The company now makes 7- and 10-inch scented worms that also look good. And, boy, do they catch fish.

So do PRADCO's YUM brand of scented ribbontail worms, available in 6 and 7½ inches.

YUM and Berkley, through its Gulp! label, also offer smaller finesse worms.

For clear water on a sunny day, I'll use the smaller baits, but, in general, I like to throw the longer worms, for they are more likely to produce large fish. Ten-inch worms are especially effective for night fishing during summer throughout much of the Midwest and Mid-South and for pursuit of double-digit bass in Florida, Texas, and Mexico.

As for color, I don't get caught up in buying dozens of variations. Instead, I think in terms of shades. I often go with natural-looking watermelon in clear water and/or when the fish are finicky. Other times, I'll throw darker worms in red shad, June bug, or black and blue.

Of course, if I'm fishing with a local expert who recommends something specific, I'll go with his suggestion.

5. YUM Dinger by PRADCO

Yes, I do like YUM products.

As with suspending jerkbaits, many good "do-nothing" soft stickbaits are on the market. I like this one, especially the 7-inch version in watermelon candy and pearl with silver flake.

And as with the others, fishing wacky-style with the Dingers can get expensive when the fish are biting. One aggressive bite or leap can tear the bait off the hook.

To prolong the life of your Dinger or any other soft stickbait, roll a small rubber O-ring or doubled-up rubber band to the middle of the body and push your hook under that. Or use a thin strip of duct tape. With any luck, you'll catch a dozen or more fish before you must replace the bait.

6. Offset Sam
by Sam Griffin

Probably you've never heard of this one, but this wooden bait by Florida lure maker Sam Griffin is my favorite topwater. It prompts ferocious explosions that leave your heart racing and your hands shaking.

I've watched guides stand open-mouthed and speechless after seeing an attack on an Offset Sam for the first time.

In fact, I've reached the point with this bait where I fish mostly

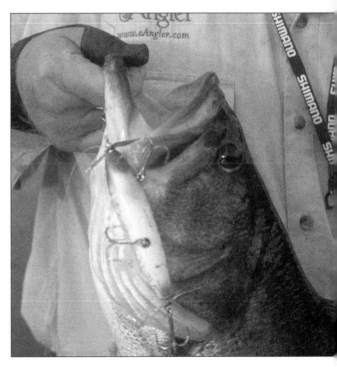

The Offset Sam topwater bait provokes savage strikes from big bass.

for the strikes instead of hooking and landing the bass. I'm addicted to the excitement. Time after time, I've seen bass jump totally out of the water to land on this bait with a stunning "kersplash!" Other times, they attack from below and charge high into the air with the bait in their mouths.

Offset Sam is a "slush" bait. With props at the head and tail, it throws up lots of spray as it cuts loudly across the surface. Bass typically hit when it is paused.

"Offset" refers to the fact that the middle set of trebles is placed to the side of the belly. Sam, also a guide on Lake Okeechobee, believes that this placement enhances hookups, and I believe him.

I like the white with black back and white with green back.

You can buy the Offset Sam and other types of Sam's topwaters directly from the lure maker at 863-946-1962.

The Spook is available in a variety of sizes and colors.

7. Zara Spook by Heddon

This is my second favorite topwater. As someone who loves to fish on top, that means I use this one often also, with variations ranging from the 3-inch Zara Puppy for stream smallmouths to the 5-inch Super Spook with saltwater hardware for peacock bass in South America.

My favorite is the 3⅛-inch Spook Jr., also with saltwater hooks. For me, it's easier to walk than the longer Spooks, and big fish seem to like it just as well. In fact, I have one that has caught at least 100 bass over 5 pounds. It used to be white with a red head, but now it is mostly clear plastic with a hint of red.

I also like the Super Spook and Spook Jr. in chartreuse with black head and black with chartreuse glitter.

For the freshwater Zara Spook and Zara Puppy, I like clear, bone, flash bass, and flash shad colors.

8. WildEye Swim Shad by Storm

Outside of California and Mexico, swimbaits were slow to gain in popularity, but now they are one of the most popular lure categories. In the wake of the long-forgotten Sassy Shad, Storm's version led the way.

Bass swim up behind these funny-looking baits and inhale them, especially the smaller 3- and 4-inch versions. Bigger bass often prefer the 5- and 6-inch models, which are harder to throw and tear up easier. But those are small negatives compared to the rewards.

I've caught dozens of 8- and 9-pound bass, as well as a couple of 10s, on these bigger baits.

Anglers can pull them along the bottom or swim them higher in the water to catch suspended bass. My favorite colors are pearl, shad, and shiner chartreuse and silver.

Big Bass Wisdom

The topwater bite was one of the most explosive that Dave Burkhardt had ever seen. At first, he feared that an alligator had grabbed his soft jerkbait, as he and friend Paul fished a Florida oxbow lake.

But then he saw a huge fish tail.

Or did he?

Two hard runs left him uncertain, as whatever was on the end of his line streaked through maidencane and out into open water. It actually towed the johnboat for a short distance, before veering back into the weeds.

As Paul steadied the boat, Dave stood and cautiously applied as much pressure as he dared, slowly gaining back his 15-pound line.

"Finally, though, she would come no higher and I knew that the line would break if I tightened the drag more or pulled any harder," Dave remembers.

Whatever was on the end of his line now was mired in the weeds below.

"That's when I put the rod down and reached down into the dark water."

Fearful that he might be reaching for a toothy bowfin, snapping turtle, or alligator, the Florida angler, nevertheless, could not resist the desire to find out what he had hooked.

In the water up to his shoulders, he finally felt the shank of his wide-gap hook and knew that he was but inches away from whatever he had hooked. The knowledge energized him and he plunged farther . . .

Somehow, he managed to lock both thumbs into an enormous mouth and, without falling overboard, wrestled aboard a true fish of a lifetime.

Following quick measurements and a couple of photos, Dave released a largemouth bass that was 28 inches long and 21 inches in girth. Weight calculated on those statistics was 15 pounds, 2 ounces, good

Big-bass expert Dave Burkhardt says that you should match your tackle and baits to the size of the fish that you want to catch.

enough for the 20-pound line-class record in the Freshwater Fishing Hall of Fame.

"When I set her back into the water, she gave a powerful flick with her tail and was gone," he says. "I collapsed onto my seat and willed my heart to slow down. My hands shook so that I couldn't retie for half an hour."

And a few years later, Dave did it again. This time he caught a 15-pound, 2-ounce bass on a spinnerbait, while fishing out of Anglers Inn on Mexico's Lake El Salto. He's also caught a 14 and a 13-pound, 8-ounce at El Salto. I was with him when he caught the latter on a crankbait.

During the fall and winter of 2007, Dave caught three 10-pounds-plus bass in Florida grove lakes.

"I've been blessed," he says simply.

But he also knows how to fish for big bass. In fact, he's the best I know. That's why I asked him to share his secrets in this book.

Here you have this privileged information in his own words:

"If you are going to fish for big bass, you have to keep big fish in mind when considering your equipment. You want a reel with a drag that will still operate smoothly when you crank it down to near the line's breaking strength. If you set it too tight, though, you could break the line or tear the hook out of the fish. And you want a rod with some backbone, but something that you are comfortable with.

"For line, I'd stay away from braid because of its knot strength. It's only about 65 to 70 percent, compared to 90 percent with other types of lines. Braid also has a definite profile in the water. You can see it against all kinds of backgrounds.

"I'd go with 15- to 20-pound. My favorite is Triple Fish 15-pound fluorocarbon. With fluorocarbon, I've seen it time and again that I can fish from the back of the boat and keep up [catching fish] with the guy in the front if I'm using fluorocarbon. It has the same light prismatic effect and so it virtually disappears. Also, it's denser than other kinds of lines, so there's a better sense of feel.

"I'd use a Palomar knot. Wet it before you pull it tight."

Next, examine what you plan to tie on the end of your line.

"Look at your baits. Look at the hooks and the split rings. What would happen if you hooked a big bass on the bait that you have in your hand? Would you land the fish or lose it? How sharp are your hooks?

"I use 5/0 heavy-shank hooks. [For soft plastics. Burkhardt has caught many of his double-digit bass on worms and soft jerkbaits.] You don't want to go to a gunfight with a knife. And you still can catch small fish on big hooks.

"I seldom use anything smaller than a 10-inch worm, and I put a rattle in it. That's a confidence thing for me."

Now it's time to go fishing.

"You want to be mentally ready for a big fish. When you do hook one, you want to remain as calm as possible and do the right things.

"Keep her down as you fight her. Keep her off the motor. You might not be able to control her in the beginning, but still you don't want to tangle your line in the prop.

"Don't tighten the drag. You should have it cranked down already. If you tighten it more, her body mass could tear the hook from her mouth. And even if you have the perfect hookup in the mandible, you can break the line if the drag is too tight.

"Having the right equipment and mental approach both are important, and so is fishing in lakes that have big bass. But I'm not a fanatic about it. I keep it fun. I don't want to fish five days for one bite.

"The most important thing is to be prepared for that big bite. It's a thought process."

Elephants Eat Peanuts

And speaking of being prepared, that's what enabled Barry St. Clair to catch the Texas state record largemouth bass while he was fishing for crappie on January 24, 1992.

As a bass angler, you've probably already heard the most compelling part of the story: St. Clair caught the 18.18-pound bass on a 1½-inch minnow.

But now you will learn the rest of the story.

St. Clair had been bass fishing on Lake Fork with two friends. They decided to stop and catch a few crappie for the table. St. Clair didn't have light tackle with him, so he simply put 12 inches of 8-pound leader and a 1/0 gold Aberdeen hook onto his bass rod and reel, which was loaded with 14-pound line.

The strength of that line and the backbone of the rod played no small part in the battle that was about to occur.

"At first, I didn't know what I had," St. Clair told me. "But I never panicked. That's what helped me get the fish in.

"I put pressure on it, and it started to move. Right away, I thought it might be a big catfish. But it didn't act like a catfish."

The fish ran three times, but stayed deep. "I took the time to wear her out," St. Clair said. "Then I eased her toward the surface."

"When she came up, it was like an exploding buoy coming out of the water. We all were stunned. Then I screamed 'Get the net!' at my buddies."

Once he had her in, St. Clair noted that the big bass "filled the bottom of the boat," and he saw that the delicate wire hook was bent nearly into a circle. "One more run and she would have been gone," he said.

Since that memorable day, the man who works as an educational specialist at the Texas Freshwater Fisheries Center has learned that his experience was not unique.

SECRET In other words, big bass will eat little baits, just as elephants will munch peanuts.

"I've run across numerous examples of others who were doing the same thing [crappie fishing] when they hooked something big," he said. "A few got them in and the fish were in the 13-pound range. Others couldn't do it. I was lucky I had tackle stout enough to handle the fish."

Here's another example of a big bass dining at the hors d'oeuvres tray instead of the buffet table: In April 2006, Randy Beaty, Jr. used a ⅛-ounce Blakemore Roadrunner to catch a 15.68-pound bass at Florida's Bienville Plantation.

And my personal favorite: I caught a 12-pound, 4-ounce largemouth bass on a ⅜-ounce Cordell Spot, while fishing in Mexico's Lake Guerrero. In case you're not familiar with it, that lipless crankbait is a mere 3 inches long, seemingly hardly an appetizer for a big bass.

Why do big bass sometimes eat little baits?

SECRET Well, luck does play a factor. Maybe St. Clair, Beaty, and I just threw our baits in the right place at the right time. A big bait might have worked as well.

In truth, few, if any, anglers know how to consistently pattern big bass with small baits. Most fisheries biologists and anglers subscribe to the theory that natural selection favors predators that maximize the efficiency of their capture of prey. In other words, a big bass should be looking to eat the largest prey possible with the least amount of energy expended to catch it.

But here are some variables to keep in mind:

A slow-moving small bait can require less energy to catch than a fast-moving large bait. In clear water, where a big bass can see better, it might not be as apt to reject a small bait, which is less defined, than a large offering, which can be more easily seen and possibly rejected.

If the most abundant forage is small, that might be what big bass are keying on.

SECRET "Match the hatch" applies to bass fishing as well as trout fishing, where the term originated with insect hatches. If you see bass feeding on small forage, throw a bait that matches that size.

SECRET And don't forget that big bass are different. They've lived longer and seen more than their smaller brethren. They've watched countless supersize jigs and worms bouncing, crankbaits swimming, and topwaters popping. Maybe a never-before-seen peanut bait is just what a lunker needs to get its juices flowing.

Trophy Tactics

While targeting big bass with small baits may be a bit problematic, you can increase your odds of landing a lunker.

Here's a big-bass pattern shared by Bruce Holt, executive director of the G.Loomis fishing rod company, who fishes as often as possible in the lakes of Mexico. He used this method to catch a 13-pound, 5-ounce trophy:

"The soft jerkbait is an excellent bait early in the spring when the big females are out cruising the shoreline, checking out the shallow-water conditions as Mother Nature's clock tells them the spawning season is coming soon.

"While a lot of anglers are fishing jigs on the drop-offs and secondary points, I like to fish a white Super Fluke on the inside edges of flat points and short bays near deep water. I rig it on a 5/0 Gamakatsu, extra-wide-gap, Superline worm hook. It may look a little out of balance, but it casts well and it helps keep the bait just a little deeper. I don't want the Fluke to pop up to the surface like all soft plastic jerkbaits have a tendency to do. I want to keep it down in the strike zone.

"And if I'm lucky enough to hook a really big bass, I can put a lot of pressure on it without fear of the hook straightening. I fish 20-pound Stren Magna-Thin. It's easy to cast because it has a thinner profile, yet it has plenty of strength to pull even the largest bass out of the heavy cover.

"The main advantage of fishing this style of bait is that I can throw it into any type of cover without fear of getting hung up because it is so weedless, and it sinks really slowly, which forces me to slow down. Prespawn bass are not willing to run down a bait this time of the year. They're looking for an easy meal, and the Fluke fits the bill.

"A slow presentation and patience are key factors. The tendency is to jerk the bait too much and not let the bass find it. Early spring anglers pull more baits away from willing biters than they realize. The key is to *slow down!*

Bruce Holt likes to throw a soft jerkbait during early spring, when big females are cruising the shoreline.

"Early in the year, the big females will stage on secondary points with a propensity to move shallow now and then. They aren't necessarily locked on any specific piece of structure. They are more interested in potential spawning areas, or flat areas near deep water, where they'll cruise along the shore for brief periods and then slide back off the edge and hold on a comfortable breakline.

"The slow drift-pause-drift approach is best. Don't jerk the bait. Allow it to sink. Let it just hang there or even go to the bottom. When you do move it, move it slowly with short pulls of the rod tip. Watch your line because the takes are usually *very* subtle. Sometimes you won't even feel it. The fish will just slowly swim off, and you'll see rather than feel your line move a bit. Sometimes there's a distinctive 'thunk,' especially with smaller fish, but the important thing is to jerk quickly and hard. Not only do you have to drive a thicker-than-normal hook into the jaw of a big fish, but you've got to pull it through all that plastic as well.

"To set the hook, I drop the tip and snap. That allows me to develop high rod-tip speed that shocks the hook through the bait and into the bass's mouth quickly. At the same time, it confuses the fish, allowing me to pull it from heavy cover before it can react.

"My rod of choice is a 7-1 GLX Jig & Worm Series, medium-heavy casting rod from G.Loomis. It has a light enough tip to cast the bait, with plenty of power in the lower section of the rod to set the hook. It is extremely sensitive and gives me a distinct advantage when the bite is subtle, and it's about as light in weight as a rod can get."

SECRET Go to waters noted for producing big bass. In Florida, that includes Stickmarsh, Kissimmee, and Toho, among others. In Texas, some of the best include Amistad, Choke Canyon, Falcon, and Rayburn, as well as Lake Fork. Don't forget the lakes of southern California and Mexico.

Can't afford the expense or time away? Look to farm ponds, many of which receive little or no pressure.

SECRET Just as important as picking the right lakes is choosing the right locations within those waters.

Offshore is the top choice for Tim Horton, BASS 2000 Angler of the Year. "It seems most people fish the banks," he says. "Big bass tend to avoid heavily fished areas."

Florida pro Bernie Schultz likes a mix of cover, as well as isolated hideaways, such as "lonely" docks, cypress trees, or small clumps of grass away from a main grass bed.

"Bigger bass are sometimes rogues, and isolated cover seems to hold

Offshore waters are less heavily pressured, and therefore could be good places to find a trophy.

them," he explained. "Plus, there is usually less pressure on these out-of-the-way places."

SECRET Especially in the South, fish the prespawn and the spawn, when big females are heaviest. But if you are going to Florida or eastern Mexico, be aware that a cold front can delay the migration to shallow water, drive fish deep again if they already had moved into the shallows, and/or give them lockjaw for several days.

Farther north, where cold weather is more consistent, winter can be a good time for catching big northern-strain largemouths.

SECRET Yes, bass will eat small baits, but throwing a big bait will improve your odds of catching a trophy. Big jigs, swimbaits, and spin-

"Lonely" docks in less pressured areas sometimes hold big fish.

nerbaits are some of the best options, as are 10- to 12-inch worms and hefty topwaters, such as the Heddon Super Spook and Offset Sam.

(Live) Food for Thought

SECRET Try a shiner.

Live-bait fishing for big bass once was considered a blood sport. Many fish died as a result of swallowing big shiners and being gut-hooked, especially by less skilled anglers. Circle hooks, however, have changed all that. Fish don't swallow a circle (sometimes called a "round") hook. Instead, as the angler lifts the rod, the hook rotates to the side of the fish's mouth and sticks there.

Dave Precht, my good friend and editor-in-chief at *Bassmaster,* has enjoyed some of his best success with big bass while shiner fishing. In the following, he shares his insight:

"Diehard bass anglers look at you with something like disdain when you admit that your biggest bass fell for a live shiner. I've taken to calling them 'central Florida swimbaits,' but people eventually figure it out.

"Shiner fishing isn't my favorite brand of the sport. But it's the only way I know—other than bed fishing—to have a legitimate shot at a trophy bass. I've fished with live golden shiners four times in my long fishing career, and each trip produced a bass weighing more than 8½ pounds. The last two trips gave me my lifetime heaviest bass: a pair of Florida large-mouths that each weighed 11 pounds, 8 ounces on certified scales. The latter fish had already spawned. A month earlier, she might have pushed 'teen' status.

"On both trips, my companion and 'guide' was Jeffrey Smith of Blue Springs, Missouri, one of the best and most successful trophy bass hunters I've ever met. He's caught several bass over 10 pounds on artificials, but the number of giant fish he's hooked with shiners is mind-boggling.

"I didn't believe him when he first told me he catches a 10-pounder on almost every trip. I had to see that for myself. On the first outing, a two-day trip on Lake Istokpoga in south-central Florida, he put me on my first three 10-plus-pounders, including the 11-pounds, 8-ounces, while he caught four over 10, including one just over 14 pounds.

"In the spring of 2008, Smith and I fished one afternoon on a small, semipublic lake in central Florida. By lunchtime, he had a 14-pound, 4-ounce in the boat, so he let me fight the fish that harassed our shiners in the afternoon. My first two battles ended in broken 20-pound fluorocar-bon lines, but after I settled down I was able to land one fish over 9 pounds and two more over 11.

"I've caught a few 10-pounders on artificial lures in recent years, and I probably cherish those memories more because they were a testa-ment more to my skill than to the size and liveliness of the shiners. Still, the sheer power of an 11-pound bass pulling 20-pound line against a tight drag is a thrill in itself.

"The real skill is Smith's. To fish with him and his brother, Steve Smith, is to watch a polished, professional team in action. No detail is left to chance; no move is wasted. Over the years, they have refined shiner fishing to an art as well as a science. Their secrets are simple.

"They fish where big fish are most abundant, mostly in the weed-choked lakes of central Florida. They fish during the major spawning waves, especially the three or four days prior to the new moons and the full moons of January, February, and March. And they use the largest, wildest golden shiners they can acquire. The trophies they seek seem to care little for any shiner smaller than 6 inches in length. A 9-incher is al-most guaranteed to produce a 9- or 10-pound bass.

"After witnessing the Smith brothers in action, I'm convinced there's much more than luck to catching giant bass, even on shiners. I'll fish with them again, if they'll let me. It's the only way I'll have half a chance of catching what Jeffrey calls a 'teenager'—a bass over 13 pounds."

Fish Like a Pro— Even if You Aren't

*L*ike most of us, you don't want to be a professional angler. You have a good job, bills to pay, and a family to support.

But you would like to fish as well as the pros. Heck, who wouldn't?

Before I tell you the secrets that will put you on the road to making that happen, we must acknowledge and put aside two variables: talent and time.

Maybe you have as much raw angling talent as the professionals, and maybe you don't. Talent, whether to play a musical instrument or to catch a bass, is something that you're born with, and nothing that I can tell you will improve yours.

Certainly you don't have as much time to fish as the pros, because of other obligations. And spending considerable time on the water—while being supported financially by generous sponsors—is of critical importance in achieving success as a top-level angler.

With the Women's Bassmaster Tour just a few years old, that's the major difference that I've seen between male and female professional anglers. A few of the women could hold their own right now if they were fishing against the men. Most, however, simply haven't logged in the hours to put them on an equal footing with the men. Give them time, though, and that will happen. Raw angling talent, I believe, doesn't discriminate on the basis of sex.

Now, back to the business at hand of revealing to you the secrets that will help you fish like a pro. We've acknowledged that you might or might not be as talented as the pros. And we've realized that you simply can't invest the time on the water that the pros do.

Women pro bass anglers can be just as good as the men. Most, though, haven't logged nearly as many hours on the water, because the Women's Bassmaster Tour is only a few years old.

Still, if you are willing to make the commitment during the limited time that you do have, you can fish like a pro.

SECRET Casting precision is one of the major differences between the pros and the rest of us.

Put an old tire in the backyard, tie a casting weight or a hookless bait on the end of your line, and practice, practice, practice. Throw overhand, sidearm, and underhand, as well as flip and pitch. Instead of squeezing in a couple of hours at the lake trying to catch bass, focus solely on your presentation. It will be worth the investment.

If you've never been fishing with a pro, trust me: it is a humbling experience. The professionals throw with pinpoint accuracy. Instead of casting two or three times to nearly the same place near a stump, they pick the stump apart—front, sides, back—before moving on to the next piece of cover. And they catch the fish that the rest of us leave behind.

No one knows this better than my friend Stan Fagerstrom. As one of the world's foremost experts on casting, he has worked his monofilament magic at outdoor shows and seminars from Birmingham to Brazil and Tulsa to Tokyo. For years, he gave demonstrations, performing extraordinary feats of casting accuracy, at the Bassmaster Classic Outdoor Show.

To achieve best results from practicing in your backyard with a baitcasting reel, he says, you should acquire casting weights of ¼-, ⅜-, and ⅝-ounce.

"It's the levelwind reel, of course, that contributes most of the misery when it comes to casting problems," he says. "That's one of the reasons I recommend having a ⅝-ounce casting weight. It's considerably easier for you to develop your casting skills using that heavier weight."

Start with too light a weight, he explains, and you must do the "Hungarian hammer throw" to cast it 30 feet. In addition, you are much more likely to get backlashes.

"You'll still get backlashes, even if you practice with that heavier weight, but they won't come as often," Stan says. "They won't because that ⅝-ounce weight pulls line off the reel spool so much easier. You won't have to put nearly as much effort into your practice cast. You'll be better able to concentrate on what your thumb is doing, and it's your thumb that's the real key to consistently good casting."

You must be able to cast accurately if you want to fish like a pro.

If you want to practice casting with a spinning rod, use the ¼-ounce weight, the casting expert says. The ⅜-ounce, meanwhile, is a good choice to tie on a child's spincast outfit.

"You'll likely find it difficult to obtain casting weights in a ⅝-ounce size," Stan continues. "They've been hard to locate for years."

If you can't find one, just drill an opening in the bottom of an old plastic bait, insert some BBs or split-shot, and reseal with epoxy glue.

Also, you might want to put skirts on those practice weights and/or baits. They will make it easier for you to watch the weights in flight and see where they land. That will better enable you to make adjustments to improve accuracy.

When practicing, forget about distance and focus on accuracy, says casting expert Stan Fagerstrom.

With accuracy as your foremost goal, Stan advises, forget about distance, especially in the beginning.

"Use a couple of targets. Set one at 25 feet and a second at 30 feet," he says. "Don't set them one foot farther. I'll make a promise in that regard: If you concentrate on accuracy at close targets until you get a handle on things, you'll find the ability to cast farther comes along as a fringe benefit. Do it the other way around in the beginning, putting all the emphasis on distance, and you'll spend most of your time picking at backlashes.

"None of us have much control over most of the problems we face when it comes to catching fish," Stan concludes. "We can't do a blessed thing about the weather, the barometer, the water temperature, or the wind. We can control our ability to put a lure on target time after time. We can do it through practice.

"The sooner you realize that, the sooner you'll start catching your share of the fish."

SECRET Work on your boat positioning. How you have placed yourself in relation to the cover also will determine how effective you are in putting your bait where the bass are.

"I don't mind following another guy down a bank," says Stephen Headrick, the Smallmouth Guru of Dale Hollow Lake. "I know that I will be able to position my boat better to get the bites than he did."

Many wannabe bass pros believe that "run and gun" is the way to win tournaments. Don't spend too much time at any one place. Throw a few casts at a laydown or stump, power up, and take off for the next target. The false assumption with this strategy is that more casts will translate into more bass caught.

In truth, fewer but better casts, based on casting practice and boat position, are what translates into greater success. And you still can cover a lot of water in a short time.

SECRET Get to know your electronics and use them often, especially when looking for offshore bass, forage, and structure. I've known a lot of average anglers who don't trust—and consequently don't rely on—their electronics. But I've never met a top-level pro who doesn't consider them as essential to success as rods and reels.

Consider the case of Edwin Evers, who won the Bassmaster Elite Series Empire Chase tournament on Lake Erie in July 2007:

In an event plagued with high winds and rough water, Evers caught his fish in 36 to 42 feet of water. But first he found them with his Lowrance electronics.

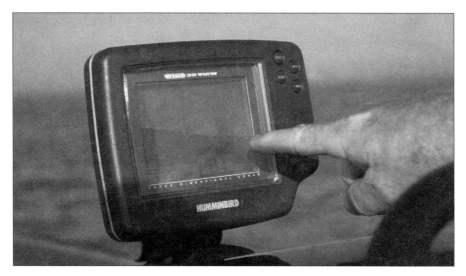

Get to know your electronics and use them often.

"I saw every fish before I caught it," he says, revealing that he also used the same tactic to finish second on Table Rock Lake.

"I think a key is that I'm just really comfortable with my electronics," he continues. "It's not catching them. It's finding them. Anyone can catch them. But you have to find the right ones."

SECRET If you are not watching your line, you are missing fish that suck in your bait and spit it out without you ever knowing.

Too many anglers mistakenly believe that all they have to do is focus on the "feel" of their rod and line and they will know when they get a bite, especially with the improved sensitively of graphite rods, tungsten weights, and fluorocarbon line.

The pros know, however, that some bites, especially when finesse fishing or flipping, are so subtle that you will not feel them, no matter how sensitive your tackle. If you don't see the subtle twitch of your line, you won't catch the fish.

One of the best ways to learn to watch your line is to go night fishing with fluorescent line and a blacklight. The darkness of the night shuts out all visual distractions outside the limited range of the light, allowing you to better focus on the line. Additionally, the night bite of a smallmouth on a jig typically is one of the subtlest that you ever will experience.

You still might not fare well against Kevin VanDam, Skeet Reese, or Ish Monroe if you improve your skills in these four areas. But you certainly will be fishing more like a pro than many who fancy themselves tournament anglers.

10

Tournament Time

The bite is slow and you wonder if you should move—again. Or maybe you should switch baits. Possibly you should slow your retrieve. Maybe speed it up.

You know that you're at least 4 pounds behind the leader and time is running short. You have only another hour before you must start back so that you can make weigh-in. Was the engine making a funny noise the last time you started it up? What if you can't make it back to the weigh-in?

Get caught on that treadmill, instead of paying attention to what you are doing, and you rarely will perform well.

A recreational angler doesn't have to worry about such complications. He can be in the moment, all of his energies directed at enticing a bass to bite. In other words, he can more easily focus.

But a tournament angler . . .

No, it's not easy, but if you want to be successful, you must focus, too. Whenever you are fishing, you must be attentive so that you can make those perfect casts, detect those subtle bites, and notice when conditions change around you.

The top pros know this and try to execute with tunnel vision on every cast. And they recognize the importance of focus in ways that might not occur to the rest of us.

While fishing a Bassmaster Classic, for example, Denny Brauer told a friend of mine that he should relieve himself when he felt the need instead of trying to hold it in. "If you don't pee when you have to, you'll be thinking about it and not paying attention to fishing," he said.

He's right, of course. The same applies to thirst, hunger, headaches, and other distractions. Don't endure them; deal with them. Then get back to focusing on catching fish.

SECRET If you're a woman, the thorny bathroom issue doesn't have to be an issue at all.

Tournament angling brings with it more distractions and can make focus more difficult.

"The easiest way to handle it is to get a poncho," says Emily Shaffer. "When the time comes, lean over the side of the boat—on the side of the boat with the steering wheel, if need be, to help you keep your balance—with the poncho covering your backside."

Or follow the suggestion of Christiana Bradley:

"My husband bought me a Little John Portable Urinal from Cabela's, and I told him thanks, but I'll never use that thing.

"I *love* it. I put it in a big plastic bag and leave it on the boat. You can squat in the bottom of the boat and throw a jacket over your rear end and have privacy, even in the most heavily pressured grass beds on the Potomac River. Nobody has a clue what you're doing."

SECRET Not all pros prefish at a tournament site. Sometimes they just drive around and study the lake. Weather and patterns often change during the time between prefishing and the tournament.

SECRET When exploring new waters, the Carolina rig is a good tool, according to pro Jan Heavener.

"Dragging the Carolina will tell me if I am fishing hard bottom, mushy with sand or sediment, chunk rock, or heavy grass. This can make a big difference. I will be able to choose the bait that will work for this type of bottom. I can also locate grass, drops, and brush."

SECRET When you catch a bass during prefishing, make note of the cover, depth, and other characteristics, and then look for similar places nearby. That can reduce the amount of time you spend traveling on tournament days.

SECRET "Strip the casing from electrical wire and slide over the hook and barb to prevent hooking fish in practice." —Rick Lillegard

SECRET Don't tie on a bait unless it is exactly what you think you should be throwing. The trebles should be sharp. If the bait is soft plastic, the hook should be straight. The lure should be the right color and shape. If it's not the best you can offer a bass, subconsciously you won't have the confidence in it that you would if it were. And that means you won't fish as well.

SECRET Don't choose a bait or pattern based on your strengths and preferences.

"When I won Angler of the Year [on the Women's Bassmaster Tour], my strategy was to do what the fish want, to let the fish dictate the pattern, instead of fishing my way," says Oklahoma pro Sheri Glasgow.

SECRET Yes, time is limited during a tournament, and you typically want to cover as much water as possible. Sometimes, though, slower is better. The better pros know this. But many beginning competitors refuse to recognize this option; they are too busy running and gunning.

And don't think that "slow" applies only to jigs and soft plastics. Sometimes, a bass won't take a suspending jerkbait while it is moving, especially in cold water.

SECRET When you are catching fish, retie often. If you don't retie after landing a fish, at least pull on the line near the bait, to make sure that it hasn't been weakened or frayed.

SECRET If you are a co-angler, and confined to the back of the boat, don't blindly throw whatever the person in front is throwing, especially if he is not catching fish. Try something different, and focus on the water that he is not fishing.

SECRET "Use a tape recorder to keep track of fish locations throughout the day." —Rick Lillegard

SECRET "Make sure your fish always have more than enough water to cover them, especially when in weigh-in line at tournaments. It's easy to begin talking about the day's events and overlook your gasping catch." —Kathy Magers

SECRET Be prepared for the unexpected.

"In my boat, I like to keep extras of certain items that especially could affect me during a tournament: extra life jacket (in case one blows out), extra bulbs, fuses, props, duct tape, jar opener or nonskid pad to loosen knobs, and heavy-duty plastic bags for transferring my catch in case of boat breakdown. If I'm using an inflatable life jacket, I'll also carry an extra cylinder," says Judy Wong.

11

Health and Fitness

*T*anya Kreuzer told me that hits to her Web site increased dramatically after I used her as my primary source in an article about health and fitness for *BASS Times*. Along with managing a construction staff in Arizona, Tanya is a long-time personal trainer and a competitor on the Women's Bassmaster Tour. Possibly that increased traffic was attributable to the fact that bass anglers are so health-conscious, especially when it comes to eating nutritious food in the boat.

Yeah, sure.

More likely, anglers—well, the male ones, at least—flocked to Tanya's site because a photo of her was included with the article. She practices what she preaches when it comes to health and fitness, and it shows.

Anglers can improve their bass fishing by better taking care of themselves, says pro angler and long-time trainer Tanya Kreuzer.

As do I, Tanya knows that many anglers tend to put health and fitness way down on the list of priorities, not realizing that such neglect hurts performance. It is *not* the way to better bass fishing.

"Eating junk food in the boat might provide you with quick energy," she says. "But it also causes your blood sugar to crash faster. That causes you to start yawning and feeling tired and lethargic.

"You might feel butterflies in your stomach, or faint, or drowsy," Tanya explains. "You might feel shaky and irritable.

"Your mind uses glucose to function and concentrate, and this is what drops when your blood sugar level drops."

SECRET Raw vegetables, fruits, nuts, string cheese, and peanut butter crackers are good fuel foods to keep you fishing at peak performance. That's because they are higher in complex carbohydrates and protein, unlike candies, chips, and cookies, which are mostly refined sugar and fat.

SECRET Don't wait until you're hungry to eat, especially if you are going fishing. You need fuel to get your body's engine moving. Too many anglers wait until they get off the water and then devour a large meal, often high in fat, before going to bed. Besides limiting performance, this habit leads to obesity.

"When you skip meals, you put your body in starvation mode," Tanya says. "Then, when you finally do eat, your body uses the nutritious components [of the meal] for energy and hordes the fat. Your body stores more of that bad food as fat because it's being starved."

SECRET Lubrication is important too. A healthy body typically requires 64 ounces of fluid a day. But when you're in the sun and sweating, you need even more. Water is the best choice, with power drinks second. Avoid drinks with lots of sugar and caffeine. The latter actually dries out your system.

SECRET On hot days, drink plenty of water *before* you get on the lake. And keep downing fluids throughout the day. If you wait until you're thirsty before you drink, you already will be feeling the weakening effects of dehydration. The weaker you are, the less attentive you will be and, thus, the less effective you will be at catching fish.

SECRET "Cold" does not quench your thirst and rehydrate your body. "Wet" does. Our obsession with having "ice cold" drinks often contributes to dehydration. That's because you can only sip a freezing beverage—unless you want to suffer brain freeze. That sip might feel refreshing, but it is not rehydrating your body. Allow that drink to warm a bit and finish it off right away, instead of putting it back in the ice chest to stay "nice and cold."

SECRET Dehydration isn't just a summer hazard. Whenever you are outdoors and active, your body needs fluid to sustain itself. Drink plenty of water in the winter, too.

Get Moving

With the increased energy that healthy eating and drinking provide, you will be more likely to consider adding exercise to your daily routine.

A simple conditioning workout, without weights, could include squats, push-ups, wrist curls, crunches, and Superman. For the latter, lie face down on the floor and then lift your arms and legs up, squeezing your muscles for three to five seconds, before release.

"For curls, squeeze your arms tight and curl them up," Tanya says. "This is an isometric contraction. For squats, lower your body slowly as if you're going to sit in a chair and hold for a few seconds. Then raise yourself back to a standing position."

These few, simple moves will make you feel better, just by getting your blood circulating, she says, adding that anyone starting an exercise routine, no matter how mild, should consult a physician first.

"If you eat properly and exercise, you are going to get much better performance from your body day in and day out," Tanya concludes.

SECRET Check out Tanya's Web site, www.bassnbabe.com, for more health and fitness tips.

SECRET "If you ever have surgery that requires exercising to mobilize a wrist, elbow, arm, or shoulder—or even chest surgery—ask the doctor if you might replace boring exercises with casting. Go fishing instead of to the gym. You can use the same muscles, and it's much more fun. Plus, natural vitamin D derived from sunshine makes you cheery."
—Kathy Magers

Bugs

SECRET Don't let that fishing trip south of the border be spoiled by a painful bite or sting. Check your shoes each morning before putting them on, to make certain that a spider, scorpion, or other critter didn't move in overnight. And watch where you step if you get up at night to go to the bathroom.

On northern waters, biting flies are often at their worst during June.

SECRET Don't wear sunglasses just to shield your eyes from glare and help you see fish in the water. Also wear them to protect your eyes from dangerous projectiles. A bug or seed can blind you if it strikes your eye while you are speeding over the water.

SECRET In Canada, Alaska, and other northern destinations, mosquitoes and biting flies usually are their most troublesome in June. But anytime that you go during the summer, be sure to take along a head net, as well as repellent.

SECRET Long-sleeved shirts and trousers will help protect you from insect bites, but they aren't foolproof. Some bugs, especially flies, will crawl up under your pants, unless you tuck the ends into your socks. Flies, gnats, and mosquitoes also will attack through those open slits on long-sleeved shirts. Be sure to put some repellent there.

Food and Drink

SECRET If you're afraid to drink the water at an exotic fishing location, then you also should avoid the ice. That's because the latter sometimes is made with tap water. Some camps and resorts do make their ice from bottled or purified water. But ask before you have that drink on the rocks.

SECRET In general, avoiding any food made with mayonnaise is a good idea during hot weather, whether you are on the water or staying at a fishing camp south of the border. Dishes such as potato, egg, and tuna salads spoil quickly in the heat, and you can't always tell that by taste. Your stomach, however, will know.

SECRET Liquid nutrition drinks are a healthy alternative to sugary soft drinks.

"I drink Ensure during practice and competition. It just takes a few seconds to slam one down," says Lance Vick. "These drinks satisfy your body's needs through the day, so your subconscious mind is not focusing on hunger. That allows you to focus on fishing."

Sun and Heat

SECRET Don't wait until you get out on the water to apply sunblock. That's bad for your health and bad for your fishing. Put it on at least a half hour before you head out, so the lotion can penetrate your skin and provide better protection. Also, this allows you to thoroughly wash your hands before you start handling your tackle. Otherwise, you'll contaminate your baits and repel the fish.

SECRET Apply plenty of sunblock to the tops of your hands and ears. Many anglers have developed skin cancer in those areas.

SECRET Put on sunblock even on cloudy or overcast days. Sun can burn you through the clouds.

SECRET Keep a handkerchief or two in your tackle or camera bag when fishing in hot climates. Soaked in water or wrapped around a piece of ice, a kerchief will cool down your whole body when you wrap it around your neck. Also, you can tuck one end up under your cap—Foreign Legionnaire style—so that the rest shields your neck and ears from the sun.

SECRET Wear a wide-brim hat if you share a small boat with a fly fisher. It will help protect your face, neck, and ears from getting hooked by an errant cast.

SECRET And on a hot summer day, with the sun beating down, exchange that baseball cap for a

Wear polarized glasses to protect your eyes from glare, as well as help you spot fish.

lightweight, wide-brim hat. Yeah, I know, it doesn't look cool. But it *is* cooler than a baseball cap because it better shades your face, ears, and neck.

SECRET Wear polarized glasses not just to see what's below the water but to protect your eyes from the sun's glare. Spending time on the water without protective glasses not only will give you headaches short-term, but cause long-term damage to your eyes.

SECRET Check out several different brands of polarized glasses before buying a pair. No two sets of eyes see exactly the same way.

SECRET Stay away from clear or light tints. Darker tints achieve greater polarizing efficiency.

12

Safety

Pam Martin-Wells decided to leave her wallet in her truck one night, while traveling east from a Women's Bassmaster Tour event at Lake Amistad. As a result, the Georgia tournament angler found herself stranded in Corsicana, Texas.

"I never leave my wallet in my truck. Never," she says. "But I did this time. And someone threw a rock through the window and stole it.

"They got credit cards, cash, everything. I didn't have any identification. If Randy Qualls of Legend Boats hadn't rescued us, I was afraid we'd be arrested for vagrancy."

On the positive side, Pam says she was overwhelmed by the generosity of those who wanted to help. "There were people I don't even know offering us money," she adds. "There's such a great camaraderie that exists in fishing."

SECRET There's also danger. If you own a fishing boat, you're a target, especially if you are on the road. Thieves know that boats often contain thousands of dollars worth of electronics and fishing tackle, as well as being valuable items by themselves. They also know that there's always the chance that the owner of the rig will get careless, as Pam was, and leave something of value in the tow vehicle.

These criminals cruise motels near interstates, as well as those at tournament sites, seeking easy marks. They frequent parking lots at launch areas, restaurants, and other places in towns around popular fishing lakes.

Even at home, however, you're at risk. "I've had my prop stolen twice out of my driveway," one pro tells me.

SECRET Most boat break-ins are crimes of opportunity. Wherever you park it, be certain that yours is not an easy target or one that encourages thieves to take a closer look.

Another pro remembers seeing two suspicious-acting strangers in a pickup truck as he parked his rig at a motel. "I had a funny feeling," he says. "I took my boat to the front and parked it right under the motel sign."

The next morning, he learned that several boats had been broken into and burglarized.

SECRET Never leave anything in plain view. "If they can't see it, they won't want it," says Steve Chaconas, a Potomac River guide who earned a college degree in criminal justice.

Chaconas also removes the sponsor logos from his truck when parking in a high-risk area. "The more logos on your truck, the more good stuff inside, and that's an invitation for the thief to pick your rig over another," he adds. "I put all of my logos on magnets and just remove them when I get to where I am staying."

Following are more tips collected from pros and guides on how to better protect your boat and tow vehicle:

1. Put locks on everything that you can put locks on, from trailer hitch to prop.

"It's amazing how many people do not lock things up," says Robin Babb, a tournament angler and former risk analyst for a security firm. "A simple lock can deter criminals because they are certain that someone else in the vicinity will not have used one. Why take the chance of someone seeing you break a lock when you can just open a door unnoticed?"

2. When possible, avoid motels that are on heavily traveled highways, poorly lit, and/or have crowded parking lots that allow thieves to work with less chance of being seen.

3. For quicker access to your boat and to keep a close eye on it, ask for a ground-floor room. Outdoor access from the room itself is much better than having to walk down a long hall to get in and out.

4. Park in a well-lighted area, preferably near your room or the motel office. You might even want to ask for a room as close to the office as possible. If you can't find a well-lighted place near your room, you're better off to park where lighting is better and your rig will be more visible.

5. When possible, back your boat up against a wall. With such placement, a thief can't cut off the hitch lock and steal the boat.

6. Always cover your boat at night. It's not much protection, but it is one more obstacle for a thief to deal with. The more barriers you erect, the better protected you are.

7. Tell motel and hotel security people where you are parking your boat and trailer, and provide your room number.

8. If you see someone suspicious around your boat, write down a description of the vehicle and its tag number.

Locks will deter criminals, says Robin Babb, pro angler and former risk analyst.

SECRET The fewer items you leave in your boat and tow vehicle, the fewer that can be stolen while you sleep. And that's not just tackle, either.

"Take in your registration, your insurance, any important papers," says Babb. "If it means something to you—and that includes electronics—take it off and take it in."

SECRET Don't spread your gear out on the deck as you prepare equipment for the next day's fishing. That shows thieves what you have and puts a big bull's-eye on your boat and vehicle.

SECRET Before you hit the road, clean out your boat. Leave behind tackle and gear that you won't need.

SECRET Don't take more than you need. Anglers are notorious for taking more tackle, especially baits, than they really need. Think twice before you load those boat storage compartments.

SECRET Don't underestimate how quickly thieves can steal. Just a few minutes at a gas station can be enough.

"I know of some guys who stopped in to pick up ice in the morning on the way to the ramp," Chaconas says. "They were inside the store just a minute but returned to find their Lowrance unit had been stolen."

SECRET "Baby monitors make good security devices to hear if someone might be tampering with your boat while you're parked at a motel." —Judy Wong

It's Personal

Your property isn't all that's at risk when you travel. Don't take unnecessary chances that will put you and your family and/or friends in harm's way.

SECRET Don't pull into a rest stop at night to take a nap. Certainly you shouldn't drive while sleepy. But if you can't afford to stay at a motel while on the road for a fishing trip, you shouldn't go.

If you must stop at night to stretch and shake off the drowsiness, do so where other people clearly are present.

"To me, the number one thing an angler should know when traveling is to be aware of one's surroundings," says Babb. "Our hurried, repetitive lifestyles can put us in almost a trancelike state in which we get into routines to make certain that we get everything done on time."

SECRET When you walk out of your motel room, don't just hop in your truck or car. Walk around it. Look inside. Check the boat. If you park at the side of a convenience store, because you could find no room out front, return cautiously.

"When we don't think about what we're doing, we put ourselves at risk without anyone else being involved," says Babb. "Now add a person who is set on doing harm or theft, and we really are in trouble."

Following are personal safety tips provided by Babb:

1. Let someone know where you are going and when you will return.
2. Have a roadside service plan in case of breakdown.
3. If you have a flat, get off the roadside and make your way carefully to a well-lit area. Don't change it in the dark.

4. If a person stops to help, stay in your locked vehicle. If you called for assistance, tell him so. Even if you don't have a cell phone, you might want to tell him that you've called if his appearance makes you nervous. If he seems genuinely concerned and you feel comfortable doing so, ask him to get help for you.

5. If you think that you are being followed or find yourself caught up in a road-rage altercation, stay calm and try to think clearly. Honk your horn and flash your lights to draw attention. Drive to the nearest well-lit location with people. A police station is best, but if you are on the road, you likely won't know where that is. Don't leave that location until you are satisfied that the follower is gone.

6. Do not immediately stop and jump out of your vehicle if you have been bumped. It may be a setup. Drive to a well-lit and populated area to exchange information with the other driver.

7. Keep a camera handy to photograph license plates, vehicles, and people whom you are uneasy about.

8. Don't show or reveal your motel room number.

9. Look around you as you exit a building or vehicle.

10. When you enter a room or vehicle, immediately lock the door.

11. Make certain that vehicle doors, motel doors, and all windows are locked.

"I believe that the most common mistake people make regarding their own security, besides not being aware of their surroundings, is not locking things up," Babb says.

12. A gun can be dangerous, even if it is yours. "It sounds empowering to own a gun," the security expert says. "But studies have found that unless you shoot regularly, are trained in hand-to-hand combat, drilled at shooting without having to think about it, and numb to subconscious consequences, the good guy will lose in a close encounter."

SECRET Travel with dowel sticks of various sizes, just in case you need them to keep a sliding glass window from opening completely, especially when running a cord through a window, says Judy Wong.

"Even when not running a cord, some windows don't line up and lock at all. I also use rubber door stops under doors with inadequate locks or for doors to adjoining rooms," she adds.

Miscellaneous

SECRET Know your insurance coverage. Many marine policies cover only the boat and accessories that are permanently attached to the hull. But insurers often will extend coverage to contents for an additional fee.

SECRET Every year, anglers drown while trying to relieve themselves from boats. While you are standing on the gunwale or near the edge, with your pants unzipped, wind or waves can send you overboard. Take along a "pee" can or bottle and relieve yourself inside the boat, where you are not as likely to lose your balance.

SECRET Such drownings also often are alcohol-related. In addition, the effects of liquor are magnified by hot weather and the rocking of the boat. Save the beer for consumption back on shore.

SECRET Wear a belt around your chest waders when stream fishing. That will keep water from filling them so quickly if you fall.

13

Favorite Bass Waters

I originally entitled this chapter "Best Bass Waters," but then I realized that my "best" is not necessarily your best. Also, no one bass lake rates as the best indefinitely. That's because weather, water levels, angling pressure, disease, exotics, and many other variables impact bass fisheries. Like rabbits, deer, and other wildlife, fish populations go through up and down cycles.

Instead, I will tell you what bass waters are my favorites and why. "Favorite" is more clearly a personal choice. Most are among the "best" that I've ever fished. A few are appealing for other reasons. Some are both.

SECRET No matter how good a bass lake is reputed to be, anglers still will experience tough days there. That's why, when booking the "trip of a lifetime," you should stay for five days, if you can afford the time and expense. That way, if a cold front moves through and shuts off the fish for a day or two, you still will have the opportunity to experience some good fishing before or afterward.

SECRET Florida strain bass are especially sensitive to cold fronts, and yes, frigid weather can extend its icy fingers way down into the Florida peninsula, as well as along the east coast of Mexico as far south as Lake Guerrero. When that happens, bass can shut off almost completely, especially in shallow, natural lakes. The good news is that cold weather down there rarely hangs on, and the bite rebounds quickly.

On the west side of Mexico, winters are more moderate and the weather more reliable.

SECRET Avoid the spawn when planning a trip to Mexico. Some outfitters will advise just the opposite. They will encourage you to go in January or February, usually prime time for spawning. Yes, fishing can be fantastic for big fish in shallow water—if you time it right. But you might not and, as a result, catch mostly small male bass because the large females haven't moved in.

Go in the fall, when bass are feeding actively, both deep and shallow. Or go in the spring or early summer, when they are concentrated deep and you can catch them on soft plastics, big crankbaits, heavy spinnerbaits, and swimbaits.

El Salto

I'd rather fish El Salto for bass than any other lake in the world. I like it for a number of reasons, not the least of which is the fishing. I've caught most of my 10-pound bass there, as well as dozens of 8- and 9-pounders.

No, the fishing isn't always the best there. Like most lakes in Mexico, it's impacted by fluctuating water levels brought about by tropical storms, drought, and irrigation. During the 10 years that I've been going there, I've seen some slow periods. But those down times don't last long and, for me at least, a slow day at El Salto still is better than a great day at most lakes. With the mountains as a backdrop, gorgeous sunsets, and icy margaritas and a relaxing massage waiting for you when you return to the resort each evening, it's just a wonderful place to be.

For me, that resort can be only Anglers Inn, owned and operated by Billy Chapman, Jr. Accommodations, meals, and staff all are first-class.

Big bass at El Salto will strike a variety of offerings, including swimbaits, spinnerbaits, big crankbaits, and soft jerkbaits.

Anglers Inn might cost a little more than other bass-fishing resorts in Mexico, but it definitely is worth it.

Plus, El Salto is easy to access compared to many other lakes in Mexico. Depending on traffic, it's just a little more than an hour's drive from the Mazatlan airport, on a paved road. Reaching some lakes, including Huites and Comedero, can require three hours or more, with much of that time spend on bumpy gravel roads.

If you decide to give El Salto a try, take 5-inch Storm WildEye swimbaits, ¾- to 1-ounce spinnerbaits, and 10-inch Berkley Power Worms in black with a blue tail. Chappy, Billy's son, says that those three produce most of the big fish, with the swimbait probably the most effective.

"Because of its weight, the swimbait is easy for a bass to spit out," he says. "When a hit comes, snap your rod tip straight up. Don't swing it off to the side." A proper hookset gives you a much better chance of sticking the bass in the upper jaw, he adds.

Favored colors include golden mullet, bunker, white, and white and chartreuse.

Chapman also recently opened an Anglers Inn at Lake Mateos, about 2½ hours to the north. At 55,000 acres, Mateos is more than twice the size of El Salto, and receives considerably less angling pressure. First report has been that it is yielding good numbers of quality (3 to 8 pounds) fish, with many coming on top. A few double-digit bass have been caught, but not yet as many as are recorded regularly at El Salto, Baccarac, and other Mexico big-bass fisheries. Likely that will improve as Chapman and his guides learn more about the lake.

You can find out more about both Anglers Inn resorts at www.anglersinn.com.

And if you decide to go to El Salto, here's a special offer only for readers of *Better Bass Fishing*: When you make your reservations, tell a member of Billy's friendly staff that you read about his resort in my book and you'll receive free a massage package ($55 value) and a selection of soft plastics that are best for fooling those big Mexico bass.

Guerrero

About 3½ hours south of the border along the east coast, Lake Guerrero could be the best bass lake in the world. That's because it is rich with grass, standing timber, shallow backwaters, and deepwater refuges, and blessed with a long growing season. The problem is that Guerrero traditionally has been subjected to extreme drawdowns, drying up much of that cover and habitat.

In general, it's more of a numbers lake. But I've caught a 12-pound, 4-ounce there, and my friend Norm Klayman boated two ten pounders.

It's worth a trip, but check on the water level before you go. And be wary of going during January and February, when a cold front can shut down the fishing and make a day on the water miserable.

I recommend Hacienda Las Palmas (www.sportsresorts.com) and Hacienda Santa Fe (www.trophyfishingetc.com).

Dale Hollow

Although Dale Hollow on the Kentucky-Tennessee border yielded the world-record smallmouth bass (11-15) in 1955 and at least two additional 10-pounders since, it's one of the most underappreciated bass fisheries

Try the float-and-fly during winter for big smallmouth bass on Dale Hollow.

today. That's because Dale Hollow's production of big fish slowed down in the 1980s and 1990s, and many anglers have yet to discover—or rediscover—it.

It is absolutely one of my favorites, and that's largely because of the 16- to 21-inch protective slot limit imposed in 2000. On a typical day, you won't catch great numbers of bass, but those that you catch will be quality fish, with a 3-pound or better average not unusual. I've caught plenty of 5-pounders there.

Dale Hollow boasts good populations of largemouth bass, walleye, and crappie as well in its clear, deep waters. Plus, it's beautiful, with rocky bluffs and thick forests along its shorelines.

You won't ever find the lake crowded with anglers, but if you go in summer, you will encounter lots of traffic from ski boats and other pleasure craft. But night fishing can be terrific.

Better yet, go in winter and try the float-and-fly technique popularized at Dale Hollow and other nearby waters. Guide Bobby Gentry (www.bobbygentry.com) will be happy to teach you the light-tackle presentation.

Whether you want to rent a cottage or a houseboat, I recommend Hendricks Creek Resort (www.hendrickscreek1.com) on the Kentucky side. It's just a few miles north of the Celina One-Stop, home of Stephen Headrick, the Smallmouth Guru, and his Punisher Lures Company. The One-Stop contains one of the best tackle stores for miles, and right next door is a barbecue restaurant that I always visit at least a couple of times when I go to Dale Hollow.

Door County

This peninsula that juts off the main part of Wisconsin to form Green Bay in Lake Michigan contains dozens of bays and inlets on both sides that are exploding with aggressive smallmouth bass. And these waters receive little pressure.

During one incredible day with guide Dale Stroschein (www .wackywalleye.com), we caught 80 to 100 smallmouths in one small bay. Most of them weighed between 3 and 4 pounds, but at least 10 of them weighed more than 5 pounds.

Weather is the limiting factor here. Winds can quickly churn up the water, making it tough to fish. But when conditions are right, this is an awesome fishery.

Big smallmouth bass frequent the many protected bays and inlets on both sides of Door County, Wisconsin.

Potomac River

Our nation's most famous river actually yielded a 10-pound bass a few years ago, but mostly it's a numbers fishery. Still, it's fun to fish the vast grass beds, wrecks, and creeks, especially with Washington-area landmarks such as the Pentagon and Mount Vernon as a backdrop. Additionally, chances improve each year that you'll hook into a big, hard-fighting snakehead while fishing for bass.

I recommend guide Steve Chaconas at www.nationalbass.com. Along with being an excellent angler and teacher, he's a great source of historic information about the area.

Florida

Florida's best bass lakes include Stickmarsh/Farm 13, Tohopekaliga on the Kissimmee Chain, Walk-in-Water, and Okeechobee. If you go after trophy bass in Florida, however, remember that many of the guides there use live shiners instead of artificials.

For fishing most of the big-fish waters, especially from Orlando south, I recommend Pete Matson (www.a1bassguideservice.com).

The Sunshine State offers an abundance of quality bass waters.

In Crystal River, anglers can catch bass and saltwater fish, including seatrout, on the same baits.

My favorite fishery in Florida, however, is not one noted for trophy bass. Yes, it contains plenty of largemouths, typically in the 2- to 4-pound range. But you're just as likely to hook into a redfish, seatrout, or jack crevalle as you are a bass.

That variety is what I like so much about the Crystal River in Citrus County on the west side of Florida.

Some bass anglers might dislike Crystal River because so much of it is a manatee preserve, and boats must stay at idle speed in those areas. But that's one of the attractions for me. If swimmers aren't harassing them, manatees will come right up to your boat. Too often, though, those who profess to love them are chasing them all around, making the big marine mammals nervous, even though Florida conservation officials strongly discourage people from touching them.

Texas

Lake Fork is the closest thing yet to a "big-bass factory." The east Texas lake just keeps producing, and definitely is worth a visit if you want to catch a trophy bass within the United States.

What many anglers don't realize, however, is that other good lakes are nearby. I recommend Palestine, Lake o' the Pines, and Bob Sandlin. They all yield big fish from time to time.

While you are in the area, stop by the Texas Freshwater Fisheries Center (www.tpwd.state.tex.us) at Athens. It's the home of the Budweiser Sharelunker Program, as well as a museum and fishing hall of fame. Chances are that you'll learn something there to improve your bass fishing.

Down along the border, Falcon and Amistad are big-fish factories when the Rio Grande carries enough flow to keep the water levels up.

California

In lakes such as Castaic and Casitas, southern California has some of the best big-bass fisheries in the nation. But unless you live within a few hours' drive, you'd be better served to go to Florida, Texas, or Mexico. These are small, heavily pressured lakes, with limited access, and those who catch the biggest bass in these clear waters are skilled specialists.

Elsewhere

Forty-nine of the 50 states boast bass fisheries. Only Alaska does not have a population of the world's most popular gamefish.

Chances are you live not far from a farm pond, or a state or municipal lake that receives little or no bass-fishing pressure. Many of these little waters are fished primarily by anglers dunking worms under bobbers and looking to catch anything that swims by. In other words, the bass likely are unschooled and vulnerable to artificials. I've caught plenty of 3- to 5-pound bass in the small waters of Missouri, my home state, with my best an 8-pounder that engulfed a buzzbait right at my feet as I walked the shoreline.

14

Conservation
and Management

When you buy fishing tackle, you help make fishing better for all of us. I'm not kidding. You might want to show this chapter to your significant other to prove what an altruistic person you are.

SECRET Under a federal program known as the Sport Fish Restoration Act (also Wallop-Breaux), excise taxes and import duties are collected on fishing equipment, motorboat and small engine fuels, and pleasure boats. That money then is distributed to the states by the U.S. Fish and Wildlife Service, with the amount each state receives based upon its number of license holders, as well as its land and water area. In 2008, more than $350 million went to the states for fisheries management and research, public access improvements, boating safety, and aquatic education.

SFR arguably is the most successful "user pays, user profits" program in the nation's history. Yet few anglers know about it.

To manage their fisheries, states rely primarily on those federal funds, as well as license fees.

"We have a statement in one of our agency documents that states that 90 percent of the funding for fishing and hunting comes from license dollars and federal excise tax revenue," says Bill Reeves, Tennessee fisheries chief. "Anyone can easily understand from this statement that virtually no program would exist without these funding sources.

"A few, very fortunate states have additional funding sources, but I feel confident in saying that Tennessee has plenty of company at the 90 to 100 percent level."

Missouri and Arkansas are rare exceptions, with a percentage of sales tax dedicated to conservation. A few others receive revenues from

To reduce delayed mortality, handle and release bass gently.

lotteries and gambling, or offer income tax check-off options. Some sell special license plates.

So keep buying that fishing tackle. It's your civic duty.

Just as important, be a watchdog. Keep an eye on what your state is doing with its share to make certain that the money is being used efficiently and appropriately.

And don't let greedy members of Congress steal those funds for other purposes. The excise taxes and import duties are "dedicated" for fisheries. But every now and then, some Washington politicians cast an envious eye on the money and try to skirt the law to get their hands on it.

SECRET We're still losing too many bass to delayed mortality following tournaments.

Yes, I know, those dead fish are "yours" anyway, your legal limit. You have a right to keep them and/or kill them. So what's the problem?

The problem mostly is one of public perceptions and public relations. Dead fish floating up around docks and along shorelines following a tournament damage the image of competitive fishing. We already have plenty of people opposed to tournament angling on "their" public waters, and this just provides them with more ammunition.

Also, fish kills from delayed mortality are wasteful and hypocritical coming from a constituency that preaches catch-and-release. Isn't the point of catch-and-release to turn fish back so that they can be caught again?

Probably we never will be able to eliminate delayed mortality completely. But there are ways to reduce the number of fish that die days or even weeks following a tournament.

1. Don't organize or participate in weigh-in tournaments that take place during the hottest part of the year. That's when bass are most stressed because of high temperatures, and most likely to contract bacterial infections from improper handling. "Paper" tournaments, where fish quickly are measured, photographed, and released at boatside, are the way to go if you must compete during summer and early fall.

2. Handle a fish as little as possible with your hands. And if you must handle it, wet your hands first. Dry hands are more likely to remove the protective slime, which prevents skin damage and infection. Also, don't use a nylon net with knots; that too will harm the fish. Instead, use smooth rubber.

3. The lower jaw makes a good handle for holding and lifting the fish. But keep your hand and the bass in vertical alignment. Don't bend the jaw; you could break it. With bass of 5 pounds or better, use your second

hand to cradle the fish right behind the belly as you lift it and/or pose for photos.

4. If the bass has swallowed the hook, prevailing wisdom used to be that you should cut the line and leave the hook in. More and more, though, anglers are using a technique similar to the method used to remove a hook from human flesh. With the latter, you push down on the eye of the hook with one hand and use line under the bend to pop it out.

For a bass, pull the shank of the hook carefully through the gill opening and point the hook eye toward the tail. That should make the bend point toward the mouth. Then reach into the mouth with pliers and pop the hook out.

Potomac guide Steve Chaconas uses a slight variation, which, he emphasizes, has worked every time. If the bass is small, he pulls the hook through the gill opening. But if it is large enough, he keeps the hook inside, still pushing the eye toward the tail. Instead of pliers, he uses the index finger of his free hand to reach under the bend and pop out the hook.

5. Keep plenty of cool, oxygenated water in your livewell for those fish you are keeping or taking for weigh-in.

6. Read *Keeping Bass Alive*, a booklet written for BASS by fisheries experts Gene Gilliland and Hal Schramm. Send an e-mail to conservation@ bassmaster.com for more information.

SECRET Keep a few fish for the table. When you take a few small bass home from a lake that has a protected slot limit, you actually are helping make it a better fishery. For example, if resource managers have placed a 12- to 16-inch slot on bass in Lunker Lake, they want you and other anglers to keep bass of less than 12 inches. That's because the lake has too many small bass in it, and they want to thin the numbers so that the remaining fish will have more to eat and can grow faster.

Why not just a standard 12-inch minimum length limit? On some lakes, that's appropriate to protect a fishery from losing too many of its big fish, when the minimum length is paired with a bag limit of five or six. In that case, the bass don't have a problem exceeding 12 inches. But when a lake has many bass "stockpiled" at about 11 inches, then larger fish (12 to 16 inches) are scarce and need to be protected as the population is restructured. Of course, a protective slot limit also allows an angler to keep bass above the slot.

The practice of catch-and-release has helped the sport of bass fishing immensely. But it should be practiced selectively, and not blindly. Sometimes, a thinning of the herd is what's needed. When you and other anglers follow regulations that encourage you to keep a few small fish,

When landing a fish, don't use a rough nylon net with knots. A net with smooth rubber mesh will do less damage to the fish's protective slime coat.

you improve your chances of catching bigger bass in that same lake a few years in the future.

SECRET For those fish you keep, here's a mouth-watering recipe for fried fish, shared with me by my friend Norm Klayman. When Klayman was a fishing guide on Bull Shoals Lake, one of his clients gave it to him.

In a plastic bag, crush and mix together equal parts Italian bread crumbs, saltine crackers, Fritos, and flour. Dip fish chunks or fillets in beaten egg mixture, drop into bag, and shake. Fry to a golden brown.

I don't eat fried fish often, but when I do, I use this recipe, and I always use it when I'm feeding fish to guests, especially those who think that they don't like fish. It's a crowd-pleaser every time.

SECRET Adding brushpiles to your favorite bass waters might improve the fishing, but most of the time, it will *not* improve the fishery.

There's nothing wrong with improving the fishing, of course, but many anglers mistakenly believe that they are somehow contributing to the overall health of a lake by dropping brush. In truth, all that does is concentrate fish, not increase their numbers.

SECRET Not all brushpiles are the same. Deciduous trees, such as oaks, have wider spacing between their branches and thus attract more and bigger bass. Cedars have tighter spaces, making them better for crappies and bluegill.

SECRET Unless your lake has had a catastrophic loss due to disease or weather, stocking probably won't improve the fishery much, either.

Not all brushpiles are created equal. Those made with larger deciduous trees, such as oak, have larger spacing between branches and, thus, attract more and bigger bass.

That's because a body of water, like an acre of land, has a finite amount of "carrying capacity."

Just as you can grow only so much corn on that acre, you can have only so much fish biomass in that lake. The carrying capacity of the lake is determined by cover, structure, fertility of the water, amount of spawning area, and other variables. An infertile lake with little cover can't accommodate as much fish mass as can a fertile lake with lots of cover.

In a lake with little carrying capacity, stocking bass on top of the existing population is just a waste of time and effort. Those added fish might improve catch rates for a short time, but they won't contribute long-term to a better population of bass.

SECRET Fisheries are altered and often damaged by nuisance non-native species, including zebra mussels, gobies, and Eurasian milfoil.

Invasive plant species such as purple loosestrife crowd out beneficial native wetland plants, especially in the Upper Midwest and around the Great Lakes.

Others, such as purple loosestrife, smother valuable wetlands. Help stop the spread of these exotics by cleaning your boat and trailer thoroughly before moving from one lake to another. Also drain the livewells and bilges, and never release live bait into a lake or river.

SECRET Although they still don't know how largemouth bass virus (LMBV) is spread, researchers have learned that the disease can live in water. That means it could be transported from one fishery to another in a livewell or bilge. Be sure to drain all water-holding compartments before moving your boat from one lake to another.

Don't move fish from one lake to another, either. Diseases such as viral hemorrhagic septicemia (VHS) can be spread that way.

SECRET One of the best ways that you can improve bass fishing now and for the future is to join a BASS Federation Nation-affiliated club near you and volunteer to help with conservation and youth projects. Go to www.bassmaster.com/federation or call national headquarters at 877-227-7872 for more information.

15

Youth

You want to fish. I want to fish. We all want to fish.

And we want better fishing, not just for us, but for our children and their children.

The problem is that most anglers don't want to do anything to make that happen.

One in every six Americans, age 16 and over, fishes. That's 30 million people, outranking golf, tennis, football, basketball, and baseball in popularity. Include the kids, and the number climbs to more than 44 million.

With such numbers, we could be one of the most powerful political forces in the country. But we're not. We just want to be left alone to fish.

The irony is that apathy is costing us our places to fish. In recent years, judges, legislatures, lake associations, and others have begun taking them away with frightening speed.

SECRET We need advocacy, and we need it now, not only for access but for keeping our waters clean and our fisheries healthy.

Fortunately, the Texas Bass Brigade is doing something about that need. We have lots of good programs out there designed to introduce children to fishing, but this is the only one I know that teaches youth to become advocates for the resource.

"When kids finish, they know more about fish, habitat, and conservation than 80 percent of tournament anglers," says Gary Van Gelder, Bass Brigade team leader.

Just as important, they learn the necessity of using that information to become community activists, and the camp gives them ample opportunities to get over stage fright. Students participate in mock media interviews and stakeholder meetings. They produce posters and PowerPoint presentations. They write articles for publication.

WARNING

WARNING
Fish from this river
are contaminted with
dangerous levels of
organochlorines and
DIOXIN
A poison that can
cause cancer,
birth defects,
and miscarriages.
Consumption of fish
or shellfish from this
river should be
avoided.
Posted by HOPE
(Help Our Polluted Environment)
In Taylor County 584-5420

We must not only teach youngsters to fish. We must teach them to be advocates for the resource.

"It's magical, the transformation and change you see in some of these young people," says Bill Eikenhorst, a volunteer mentor. "They might be wallflowers when they come in, but they are loud and proud when they leave."

Shelbi Perry, age 15, is one of those "loud and proud" individuals. Here's what she said after attending a Bass Brigade:

"This camp was so much more to me than learning about large-mouth bass, although that's what the name suggests. It was about leadership and how we can make a difference in our community, state, and even our nation. It was also about conserving and managing our lakes and natural resources, because one day, we may not be so fortunate as to have them so readily available.

"As a society, we take water for granted, thinking that it is always going to be there, but it's not. We seem to think that wildlife can continue to live here on earth with all of the horrific changes we as humans are making each day. What we forget is that we humans thrive only because of nature, wildlife, and the natural resources of our planet. Without conservation of our natural resources, we will struggle to survive in the future."

Sadly, this wonderful program is limited by a lack of financing and volunteers to help as counselors at the camp.

If you're a Texas angler who doesn't want to get involved in the political process yourself, at least donate money to aid the program that helps tomorrow's anglers grow into passionate advocates for the resource. Heck, even if you live in North Dakota or New Jersey, donate.

Even better, start a Bass Brigade program in your state.

For more information, go to www.texasbrigades.org.

16

Conclusion

As a senior writer for *Bassmaster* magazine, I was selected to ride with Rick Clunn during the final day of a Bassmaster Classic. He was the leader going into that long, long day in August, but he didn't catch a keeper. I've been with others who weren't doing well, and their frustration clearly impacted their choices and performance.

Not Rick. He remained as steady and hardworking as ever. At the end of the day, he showed no anger, either. "Hey, it happens to everyone now and then," he told me. "No one catches fish every time."

SECRET Even though the pros have proven that bass always are biting somewhere in any given lake, *everyone* strikes out occasionally.

SECRET And even when you're not getting a bite, the bass still might be in the very area where you are fishing. The Tennessee Valley Authority proves that annually. It allows anglers to fish a blocked-off cove, and then follows up with electroshocking. If they are fortunate, the anglers catch a bass or two, while the fishery biologists shock up dozens.

So, even if you memorize every word of this book and adopt every recommendation, you still will not catch bass very time you go fishing. No one does, even on the very best bass waters.

But the information provided to you will make you a better angler and improve your odds of success. In turn, I hope that you will share what you have learned in this book and through your own experiences with others, especially children.

There's still much more for all of us to learn. Right now, at least, angling is more an art than a science. And the only way that bass fishing will be the best that it can be is if we help each other.

Index